ICC Rules for the Use of Domestic and International Trade Terms

Incoterms® 2010

by the International Chamber of Commerce (ICC)

Die Regeln der ICC zur Auslegung nationaler und internationaler Handelsklauseln

Entry into force on 1st January 2011
Gültig ab 1. Januar 2011

English-German version / englisch-deutsche Ausgabe

English (original text) / German (translation)
englisch (Originaltext) / deutsch (Übersetzung)

The Incoterms® 2010 have been approved by the International Chamber of Commerce (ICC) in English. Should the German translation be inconsistent with the original English version, then the English version has priority.

Die Incoterms® 2010 sind von der Internationalen Handelskammer (ICC) in englisch verabschiedet worden. Sollte die deutsche Übersetzung zur englischen Fassung im Widerspruch stehen, so hat die englische Version Vorrang.

ICC
International Chamber of Commerce
The world business organization

CONTENTS

INCOTERMS® 2010

INHALTSVERZEICHNIS

INCOTERMS® 2010

FOREWORD

By Rajat Gupta, ICC Chairman

The global economy has given businesses broader access than ever before to markets all over the world. Goods are sold in more countries, in larger quantities, and in greater variety. But as the volume and complexity of global sales increase, so do possibilities for misunderstandings and costly disputes when sale contracts are not adequately drafted.

The Incoterms® rules, the ICC rules on the use of domestic and international trade terms, facilitate the conduct of global trade. Reference to an Incoterms® 2010 rule in a sale contract clearly defines the parties' respective obligations and reduces the risk of legal complications.

Since the creation of the Incoterms rules by ICC in 1936, this globally accepted contractual standard has been regularly updated to keep pace with the development of international trade. The Incoterms® 2010 rules take account of the continued spread of customs free zones, the increased use of electronic communications in business transactions, heightened concern about security in the movement of goods and changes in transport practices. Incoterms® 2010 updates and consolidates the 'delivered' rules, reducing the total number of rules from 13 to 11, and offers a simpler and clearer presentation of all the rules. Incoterms® 2010 is also the first version of the Incoterms rules to make all references to buyers and sellers gender-neutral.

The broad expertise of ICC's Commission on International Commercial Practice, whose membership is drawn from all parts of the world and all trade sectors, ensures that the Incoterms® 2010 rules respond to business needs everywhere.

ICC would like to express its gratitude to the members of the Commission, chaired by Fabio Bortolotti (Italy), to the Drafting Group, which comprised Charles Debattista (Co-Chair, UK), Christoph Martin Radtke (Co-Chair, France), Jens Bredow (Germany), Johnny Herre (Sweden), David Lowe (UK), Lauri Railas (Finland), Frank Reynolds (US), and Miroslav Subert (Czech Republic), and to Asko Raty (Finland) for assistance with the images depicting the 11 rules.

INTRODUCTION

The Incoterms®[1] rules explain a set of three-letter trade terms reflecting business-to-business practice in contracts for the sale of goods. The Incoterms rules describe mainly the tasks, costs and risks involved in the delivery of goods from sellers to buyers.

How to use the Incoterms® 2010 rules

1. Incorporate the Incoterms® 2010 rules into your contract of sale

If you want the Incoterms® 2010 rules to apply to your contract, you should make this clear in the contract, through such words as, "[*the chosen Incoterms rule including the named place, followed by*] Incoterms® 2010".

2. Choose the appropriate Incoterms rule

The chosen Incoterms rule needs to be appropriate to the goods, to the means of their transport, and above all to whether the parties intend to put additional obligations, for example such as the obligation to organize carriage or insurance, on the seller or on the buyer. The Guidance Note to each Incoterms rule contains information that is particularly helpful when making this choice. Whichever Incoterms rule is chosen, the parties should be aware that the interpretation of their contract may well be influenced by customs particular to the port or place being used.

3. Specify your place or port as precisely as possible

The chosen Incoterms rule can work only if the parties name a place or port, and will work best if the parties specify the place or port as precisely as possible.

A good example of such precision would be:

"FCA 38 Cours Albert 1er, Paris, France Incoterms® 2010".

Under the Incoterms rules Ex Works (EXW), Free Carrier (FCA), Delivered at Terminal (DAT), Delivered at Place (DAP), Delivered Duty Paid (DDP), Free Alongside Ship (FAS), and Free on Board (FOB), the named place is the place where delivery takes place and where risk passes from the seller to the buyer. Under the Incoterms rules Carriage Paid To (CPT), Carriage and Insurance Paid To (CIP), Cost and Freight (CFR) and Cost, Insurance and Freight (CIF), the named place differs from the place of delivery. Under these four

1 "Incoterms" is a registered trademark of the International Chamber of Commerce.

Incoterms rules, the named place is the place of destination to which carriage is paid. Indications as to place or destination can helpfully be further specified by stating a precise point in that place or destination in order to avoid doubt or argument.

4. Remember that Incoterms rules do not give you a complete contract of sale

Incoterms rules *do* say which party to the sale contract has the obligation to make carriage or insurance arrangements, when the seller delivers the goods to the buyer, and which costs each party is responsible for. Incoterms rules, however, say nothing about the price to be paid or the method of its payment. Neither do they deal with the transfer of ownership of the goods, or the consequences of a breach of contract. These matters are normally dealt with through express terms in the contract of sale or in the law governing that contract. The parties should be aware that mandatory local law may override any aspect of the sale contract, including the chosen Incoterms rule.

Main features of the Incoterms® 2010 rules

1. Two new Incoterms rules – DAT and DAP – have replaced the Incoterms 2000 rules DAF, DES, DEQ and DDU

The number of Incoterms rules has been reduced from 13 to 11. This has been achieved by substituting two new rules that may be used irrespective of the agreed mode of transport – DAT, Delivered at Terminal, and DAP, Delivered at Place – for the Incoterms 2000 rules DAF, DES, DEQ and DDU.

Under both new rules, delivery occurs at a named destination: in DAT, at the buyer's disposal unloaded from the arriving vehicle (as under the former DEQ rule); in DAP, likewise at the buyer's disposal, but ready for unloading (as under the former DAF, DES and DDU rules).

The new rules make the Incoterms 2000 rules DES and DEQ superfluous. The named terminal in DAT may well be in a port, and DAT can therefore safely be used in cases where the Incoterms 2000 rule DEQ once was. Likewise, the arriving "vehicle" under DAP may well be a ship and the named place of destination may well be a port: consequently, DAP can safely be used in cases where the Incoterms 2000 rule DES once was. These new rules, like their predecessors, are "delivered", with the seller bearing all the costs (other than those related to import clearance, where applicable) and risks involved in bringing the goods to the named place of destination.

2. Classification of the 11 Incoterms® 2010 rules

The 11 Incoterms® 2010 rules are presented in two distinct classes:

RULES FOR ANY MODE OR MODES OF TRANSPORT

EXW	Ex Works
FCA	Free Carrier
CPT	Carriage paid to
CIP	Carriage and Insurance paid to
DAT	Delivered at Terminal
DAP	Delivered at Place
DDP	Delivered Duty paid

RULES FOR SEA AND INLAND WATERWAY TRANSPORT

FAS	Free alongside Ship
FOB	Free on Board
CFR	Cost and Freight
CIF	Cost, Insurance and Freight

The first class includes the seven Incoterms® 2010 rules that can be used irrespective of the mode of transport selected and irrespective of whether one or more than one mode of transport is employed. EXW, FCA, CPT, CIP, DAT, DAP and DDP belong to this class. They can be used even when there is no maritime transport at all. It is important to remember, however, that these rules *can* be used in cases where a ship *is* used for part of the carriage.

In the second class of Incoterms® 2010 rules, the point of delivery and the place to which the goods are carried to the buyer are *both* ports, hence the label "sea and inland waterway" rules. FAS, FOB, CFR and CIF belong to this class. Under the last three Incoterms rules, all mention of the ship's rail as the point of delivery has been omitted in preference for the goods being delivered when they are "on board" the vessel. This more closely reflects modern commercial reality and avoids the rather dated image of the risk swinging to and fro across an imaginary perpendicular line.

3. Rules for domestic and international trade

Incoterms rules have traditionally been used in *international* sale contracts where goods pass across national borders. In various areas of the world, however, trade blocs, like the European Union, have made border formalities between different countries less significant. Consequently, the subtitle of the Incoterms® 2010 rules formally recognizes that they are available for application to both international and domestic sale contracts. As a result, the Incoterms® 2010 rules clearly state in a number of places that the obligation to comply with export/import formalities exists only where applicable.

Two developments have persuaded ICC that a movement in this direction is timely. Firstly, traders commonly use Incoterms rules for purely domestic sale contracts. The second reason is the greater willingness in the United States to use Incoterms rules in domestic trade rather than the former Uniform Commercial Code shipment and delivery terms.

4. Guidance Notes

Before each Incoterms® 2010 rule you will find a Guidance Note. The Guidance Notes explain the fundamentals of each Incoterms rule, such as when it should be used, when risk passes, and how costs are allocated between seller and buyer. The Guidance Notes are not part of the actual Incoterms® 2010 rules, but are intended to help the user accurately and efficiently steer towards the appropriate Incoterms rule for a particular transaction.

5. Electronic communication

Previous versions of Incoterms rules have specified those documents that could be replaced by EDI messages. Articles **A1/B1** of the Incoterms® 2010 rules, however, now give electronic means of communication the same effect as paper communication, as long as the parties so agree or where customary. This formulation facilitates the evolution of new electronic procedures throughout the lifetime of the Incoterms® 2010 rules.

6. Insurance cover

The Incoterms® 2010 rules are the first version of the Incoterms rules since the revision of the Institute Cargo Clauses and take account of alterations made to those clauses. The Incoterms® 2010 rules place information duties relating to insurance in articles **A3/B3**, which deal with contracts of carriage and insurance. These provisions have been moved from the more generic articles found in articles **A10/B10** of the Incoterms 2000 rules. The language in articles **A3/B3** relating to insurance has also been altered with a view to clarifying the parties' obligations in this regard.

7. Security-related clearances and information required for such clearances

There is heightened concern nowadays about security in the movement of goods, requiring verification that the goods do not pose a threat to life or property for reasons other than their inherent nature. Therefore, the Incoterms® 2010 rules have allocated obligations between the buyer and seller to obtain or to render assistance in obtaining security-related clearances, such as chain-of-custody information, in articles **A2/B2** and **A10/B10** of various Incoterms rules.

8. Terminal handling charges

Under Incoterms rules CPT, CIP, CFR, CIF, DAT, DAP, and DDP, the seller must make arrangements for the carriage of the goods to the agreed destination. While the freight is paid by the seller, it is actually paid *for* by the buyer as freight costs are normally included by the seller in the total selling price. The carriage costs will sometimes include the costs of handling and moving the goods within port or container terminal facilities and the carrier or terminal operator may well charge these costs to the buyer who receives the goods. In these circumstances, the buyer will want to avoid paying for the same service twice: once to the seller as part of the total selling price and once independently to the carrier or the terminal operator. The Incoterms® 2010 rules seek to avoid this happening by clearly allocating such costs in articles **A6/B6** of the relevant Incoterms rules.

9. String sales

In the sale of commodities, as opposed to the sale of manufactured goods, cargo is frequently sold several times during transit "down a string". When this happens, a seller in the middle of the string does not "ship" the goods because these have already been shipped by the first seller in the string. The seller in the middle of the string therefore performs its obligations towards its buyer not by shipping the goods, but by "procuring" goods that have been shipped. For clarification purposes, Incoterms® 2010 rules include the obligation to "procure goods shipped" as an alternative to the obligation to ship goods in the relevant Incoterms rules.

Variants of Incoterms rules

Sometimes the parties want to alter an Incoterms rule. The Incoterms® 2010 rules do not prohibit such alteration, but there are dangers in so doing. In order to avoid any unwelcome surprises, the parties would need to make the intended effect of such alterations extremely clear in their contract. Thus, for example, if the allocation of costs in the Incoterms® 2010 rules is altered in the contract, the parties should also clearly state whether they intend to vary the point at which the risk passes from seller to buyer.

Status of this introduction

This introduction gives general information on the use and interpretation of the Incoterms® 2010 rules, but does not form part of those rules.

Explanation of terms used in the Incoterms® 2010 rules

As in the Incoterms 2000 rules, the seller's and buyer's obligations are presented in mirror fashion, reflecting under column A the seller's obligations and under column B the buyer's obligations. These obligations can be carried out personally by the seller or the buyer or sometimes, subject to terms in the contract or the applicable law, through intermediaries such as carriers, freight forwarders or other persons nominated by the seller or the buyer for a specific purpose.

The text of the Incoterms® 2010 rules is meant to be self-explanatory. However, in order to assist users the following text sets out guidance as to the sense in which selected terms are used throughout the document.

Carrier: For the purposes of the Incoterms® 2010 rules, the carrier is the party with whom carriage is contracted.

Customs formalities: These are requirements to be met in order to comply with any applicable customs regulations and may include documentary, security, information or physical inspection obligations.

Delivery: This concept has multiple meanings in trade law and practice, but in the Incoterms® 2010 rules, it is used to indicate where the risk of loss of or damage to the goods passes from the seller to the buyer.

Delivery document: This phrase is now used as the heading to article **A8**. It means a document used to prove that delivery has occurred. For many of the Incoterms® 2010 rules, the delivery document is a transport document or corresponding electronic record. However, with EXW, FCA, FAS and FOB, the delivery document may simply be a receipt. A delivery document may also have other functions, for example as part of the mechanism for payment.

Electronic record or procedure: A set of information constituted of one or more electronic messages and, where applicable, being functionally equivalent with the corresponding paper document.

Packaging: This word is used for different purposes:

1. The packaging of the goods to comply with any requirements under the contract of sale.

2. The packaging of the goods so that they are fit for transportation.

3. The stowage of the packaged goods within a container or other means of transport.

In the Incoterms® 2010 rules, packaging means both the first and second of the above. The Incoterms® 2010 rules do not deal with the parties' obligations for stowage within a container and therefore, where relevant, the parties should deal with this in the sale contract.

RULES
FOR ANY MODE
OR MODES
OF TRANSPORT

EXW
EX WORKS

EXW *(insert named place of delivery)* Incoterms® 2010

GUIDANCE NOTE

This rule may be used irrespective of the mode of transport selected and may also be used where more than one mode of transport is employed. It is suitable for domestic trade, while FCA is usually more appropriate for international trade.

"Ex Works" means that the seller delivers when it places the goods at the disposal of the buyer at the seller's premises or at another named place (i.e., works, factory, warehouse, etc.). The seller does not need to load the goods on any collecting vehicle, nor does it need to clear the goods for export, where such clearance is applicable.

The parties are well advised to specify as clearly as possible the point within the named place of delivery, as the costs and risks to that point are for the account of the seller. The buyer bears all costs and risks involved in taking the goods from the agreed point, if any, at the named place of delivery.

EXW represents the minimum obligation for the seller. The rule should be used with care as:

a. The seller has no obligation to the buyer to load the goods, even though in practice the seller may be in a better position to do so. If the seller does load the goods, it does so at the buyer's risk and expense. In cases where the seller is in a better position to load the goods, FCA, which obliges the seller to do so at its own risk and expense, is usually more appropriate.

b. A buyer who buys from a seller on an EXW basis for export needs to be aware that the seller has an obligation to provide only such assistance as the buyer may require to effect that export: the seller is not bound to organize the export clearance. Buyers are therefore well advised not to use EXW if they cannot directly or indirectly obtain export clearance.

c. The buyer has limited obligations to provide to the seller any information regarding the export of the goods. However, the seller may need this information for e.g., taxation or reporting purposes.

A THE SELLER'S OBLIGATIONS

A1 General obligations of the seller

The seller must provide the goods and the commercial invoice in conformity with the contract of sale and any other evidence of conformity that may be required by the contract.

Any document referred to in **A1–A10** may be an equivalent electronic record or procedure if agreed between the parties or customary.

A2 Licences, authorizations, security clearances and other formalities

Where applicable, the seller must provide the buyer, at the buyer's request, risk and expense, assistance in obtaining any export licence, or other official authorization necessary for the export of the goods.

Where applicable, the seller must provide, at the buyer's request, risk and expense, any information in the possession of the seller that is required for the security clearance of the goods.

A3 Contracts of carriage and insurance

a. Contract of carriage
The seller has no obligation to the buyer to make a contract of carriage.

b. Contract of insurance
The seller has no obligation to the buyer to make a contract of insurance. However, the seller must provide the buyer, at the buyer's request, risk, and expense (if any), with information that the buyer needs for obtaining insurance.

A4 Delivery

The seller must deliver the goods by placing them at the disposal of the buyer at the agreed point, if any, at the named place of delivery, not loaded on any collecting vehicle. If no specific point has been agreed within the named place of delivery, and if there are several points available, the seller may select the point that best suits its purpose. The seller must deliver the goods on the agreed date or within the agreed period.

B THE BUYER'S OBLIGATIONS

B1 General obligations of the buyer

The buyer must pay the price of the goods as provided in the contract of sale.

Any document referred to in **B1–B10** may be an equivalent electronic record or procedure if agreed between the parties or customary.

B2 Licences, authorizations, security clearances and other formalities

Where applicable, it is up to the buyer to obtain, at its own risk and expense, any export and import licence or other official authorization and carry out all customs formalities for the export of the goods.

B3 Contracts of carriage and insurance

a. Contract of carriage
   The buyer has no obligation to the seller to make a contract of carriage.

b. Contract of insurance
   The buyer has no obligation to the seller to make a contract of insurance.

B4 Taking delivery

The buyer must take delivery of the goods when **A4** and **A7** have been complied with.

A5 Transfer of risks

The seller bears all risks of loss of or damage to the goods until they have been delivered in accordance with **A4** with the exception of loss or damage in the circumstances described in **B5**.

A6 Allocation of costs

The seller must pay all costs relating to the goods until they have been delivered in accordance with **A4**, other than those payable by the buyer as envisaged in **B6**.

A7 Notices to the buyer

The seller must give the buyer any notice needed to enable the buyer to take delivery of the goods.

A8 Delivery document

The seller has no obligation to the buyer.

B5 Transfer of risks

The buyer bears all risks of loss of or damage to the goods from the time they have been delivered as envisaged in **A4**.

If the buyer fails to give notice in accordance with **B7**, then the buyer bears all risks of loss of or damage to the goods from the agreed date or the expiry date of the agreed period for delivery, provided that the goods have been clearly identified as the contract goods.

B6 Allocation of costs

The buyer must:

a. pay all costs relating to the goods from the time they have been delivered as envisaged in **A4**;

b. pay any additional costs incurred by failing either to take delivery of the goods when they have been placed at its disposal or to give appropriate notice in accordance with **B7**, provided that the goods have been clearly identified as the contract goods;

c. pay, where applicable, all duties, taxes and other charges, as well as the costs of carrying out customs formalities payable upon export; and

d. reimburse all costs and charges incurred by the seller in providing assistance as envisaged in **A2**.

B7 Notices to the seller

The buyer must, whenever it is entitled to determine the time within an agreed period and/or the point of taking delivery within the named place, give the seller sufficient notice thereof.

B8 Proof of delivery

The buyer must provide the seller with appropriate evidence of having taken delivery.

A9 Checking – packaging – marking

The seller must pay the costs of those checking operations (such as checking quality, measuring, weighing, counting) that are necessary for the purpose of delivering the goods in accordance with **A4**.

The seller must, at its own expense, package the goods, unless it is usual for the particular trade to transport the type of goods sold unpackaged. The seller may package the goods in the manner appropriate for their transport, unless the buyer has notified the seller of specific packaging requirements before the contract of sale is concluded. Packaging is to be marked appropriately.

A10 Assistance with information and related costs

The seller must, where applicable, in a timely manner, provide to or render assistance in obtaining for the buyer, at the buyer's request, risk and expense, any documents and information, including security-related information, that the buyer needs for the export and/or import of the goods and/or for their transport to the final destination.

B9 Inspection of goods

The buyer must pay the costs of any mandatory pre-shipment inspection, including inspection mandated by the authorities of the country of export.

B10 Assistance with information and related costs

The buyer must, in a timely manner, advise the seller of any security information requirements so that the seller may comply with **A10**.

The buyer must reimburse the seller for all costs and charges incurred by the seller in providing or rendering assistance in obtaining documents and information as envisaged in **A10**.

FCA
FREE CARRIER

FCA *(insert named place of delivery)* Incoterms® 2010

GUIDANCE NOTE

This rule may be used irrespective of the mode of transport selected and may also be used where more than one mode of transport is employed.

"Free Carrier" means that the seller delivers the goods to the carrier or another person nominated by the buyer at the seller's premises or another named place. The parties are well advised to specify as clearly as possible the point within the named place of delivery, as the risk passes to the buyer at that point.

If the parties intend to deliver the goods at the seller's premises, they should identify the address of those premises as the named place of delivery. If, on the other hand, the parties intend the goods to be delivered at another place, they must identify a different specific place of delivery.

FCA requires the seller to clear the goods for export, where applicable. However, the seller has no obligation to clear the goods for import, pay any import duty or carry out any import customs formalities.

A THE SELLER'S OBLIGATIONS

A1 General obligations of the seller

The seller must provide the goods and the commercial invoice in conformity with the contract of sale and any other evidence of conformity that may be required by the contract.

Any document referred to in **A1–A10** may be an equivalent electronic record or procedure if agreed between the parties or customary.

A2 Licences, authorizations, security clearances and other formalities

Where applicable, the seller must obtain, at its own risk and expense, any export licence or other official authorization and carry out all customs formalities necessary for the export of the goods.

A3 Contracts of carriage and insurance

a. Contract of carriage

The seller has no obligation to the buyer to make a contract of carriage. However, if requested by the buyer or if it is commercial practice and the buyer does not give an instruction to the contrary in due time, the seller may contract for carriage on usual terms at the buyer's risk and expense. In either case, the seller may decline to make the contract of carriage and, if it does, shall promptly notify the buyer.

b. Contract of insurance

The seller has no obligation to the buyer to make a contract of insurance. However, the seller must provide the buyer, at the buyer's request, risk, and expense (if any), with information that the buyer needs for obtaining insurance.

B THE BUYER'S OBLIGATIONS

B1 General obligations of the buyer

The buyer must pay the price of the goods as provided in the contract of sale.

Any document referred to in **B1–B10** may be an equivalent electronic record or procedure if agreed between the parties or customary.

B2 Licences, authorizations, security clearances and other formalities

Where applicable, it is up to the buyer to obtain, at its own risk and expense, any import licence or other official authorization and carry out all customs formalities for the import of the goods and for their transport through any country.

B3 Contracts of carriage and insurance

a. Contract of carriage

The buyer must contract at its own expense for the carriage of the goods from the named place of delivery, except when the contract of carriage is made by the seller as provided for in **A3 a**.

b. Contract of insurance

The buyer has no obligation to the seller to make a contract of insurance.

A4 Delivery

The seller must deliver the goods to the carrier or another person nominated by the buyer at the agreed point, if any, at the named place on the agreed date or within the agreed period.

Delivery is completed:

a. If the named place is the seller's premises, when the goods have been loaded on the means of transport provided by the buyer.

b. In any other case, when the goods are placed at the disposal of the carrier or another person nominated by the buyer on the seller's means of transport ready for unloading.

If no specific point has been notified by the buyer under **B7 d** within the named place of delivery, and if there are several points available, the seller may select the point that best suits its purpose.

Unless the buyer notifies the seller otherwise, the seller may deliver the goods for carriage in such a manner as the quantity and/or nature of the goods may require.

A5 Transfer of risks

The seller bears all risks of loss of or damage to the goods until they have been delivered in accordance with **A4**, with the exception of loss or damage in the circumstances described in **B5**.

B4 Taking delivery

The buyer must take delivery of the goods when they have been delivered as envisaged in **A4**.

B5 Transfer of risks

The buyer bears all risks of loss of or damage to the goods from the time they have been delivered as envisaged in **A4**.

If

a. the buyer fails in accordance with **B7** to notify the nomination of a carrier or another person as envisaged in **A4** or to give notice; or

b. the carrier or person nominated by the buyer as envisaged in **A4** fails to take the goods into its charge,

then, the buyer bears all risks of loss of or damage to the goods:

i. from the agreed date, or in the absence of an agreed date,
ii. from the date notified by the seller under **A7** within the agreed period; or, if no such date has been notified,
iii. from the expiry date of any agreed period for delivery,

provided that the goods have been clearly identified as the contract goods.

A6 Allocation of costs

The seller must pay

a. all costs relating to the goods until they have been delivered in accordance with **A4**, other than those payable by the buyer as envisaged in **B6**; and

b. where applicable, the costs of customs formalities necessary for export, as well as all duties, taxes, and other charges payable upon export.

A7 Notices to the buyer

The seller must, at the buyer's risk and expense, give the buyer sufficient notice either that the goods have been delivered in accordance with **A4** or that the carrier or another person nominated by the buyer has failed to take the goods within the time agreed.

A8 Delivery document

The seller must provide the buyer, at the seller's expense, with the usual proof that the goods have been delivered in accordance with **A4**.

The seller must provide assistance to the buyer, at the buyer's request, risk and expense, in obtaining a transport document.

B6 Allocation of costs

The buyer must pay

a. all costs relating to the goods from the time they have been delivered as envisaged in **A4**, except, where applicable, the costs of customs formalities necessary for export, as well as all duties, taxes, and other charges payable upon export as referred to in **A6 b**;

b. any additional costs incurred, either because:
   i. the buyer fails to nominate a carrier or another person as envisaged in **A4**, or
   ii. the carrier or person nominated by the buyer as envisaged in **A4** fails to take the goods into its charge, or
   iii. the buyer has failed to give appropriate notice in accordance with **B7**,

   provided that the goods have been clearly identified as the contract goods; and

c. where applicable, all duties, taxes and other charges as well as the costs of carrying out customs formalities payable upon import of the goods and the costs for their transport through any country.

B7 Notices to the seller

The buyer must notify the seller of

a. the name of the carrier or another person nominated as envisaged in **A4** within sufficient time as to enable the seller to deliver the goods in accordance with that article;

b. where necessary, the selected time within the period agreed for delivery when the carrier or person nominated will take the goods;

c. the mode of transport to be used by the person nominated; and

d. the point of taking delivery within the named place.

B8 Proof of delivery

The buyer must accept the proof of delivery provided as envisaged in **A8**.

A9 Checking – packaging – marking

The seller must pay the costs of those checking operations (such as checking quality, measuring, weighing, counting) that are necessary for the purpose of delivering the goods in accordance with **A4**, as well as the costs of any pre-shipment inspection mandated by the authority of the country of export.

The seller must, at its own expense, package the goods, unless it is usual for the particular trade to transport the type of goods sold unpackaged. The seller may package the goods in the manner appropriate for their transport, unless the buyer has notified the seller of specific packaging requirements before the contract of sale is concluded. Packaging is to be marked appropriately.

A10 Assistance with information and related costs

The seller must, where applicable, in a timely manner, provide to or render assistance in obtaining for the buyer, at the buyer's request, risk and expense, any documents and information, including security-related information, that the buyer needs for the import of the goods and/or for their transport to the final destination.

The seller must reimburse the buyer for all costs and charges incurred by the buyer in providing or rendering assistance in obtaining documents and information as envisaged in **B10**.

B9 Inspection of goods

The buyer must pay the costs of any mandatory pre-shipment inspection, except when such inspection is mandated by the authorities of the country of export.

B10 Assistance with information and related costs

The buyer must, in a timely manner, advise the seller of any security information requirements so that the seller may comply with **A10**.

The buyer must reimburse the seller for all costs and charges incurred by the seller in providing or rendering assistance in obtaining documents and information as envisaged in **A10**.

The buyer must, where applicable, in a timely manner, provide to or render assistance in obtaining for the seller, at the seller's request, risk and expense, any documents and information, including security-related information, that the seller needs for the transport and export of the goods and for their transport through any country.

CPT
CARRIAGE PAID TO

CPT *(insert named place of destination)* Incoterms® 2010

GUIDANCE NOTE

This rule may be used irrespective of the mode of transport selected and may also be used where more than one mode of transport is employed.

"Carriage Paid To" means that the seller delivers the goods to the carrier or another person nominated by the seller at an agreed place (if any such place is agreed between the parties) and that the seller must contract for and pay the costs of carriage necessary to bring the goods to the named place of destination.

When CPT, CIP, CFR or CIF are used, the seller fulfils its obligation to deliver when it hands the goods over to the carrier and not when the goods reach the place of destination.

This rule has two critical points, because risk passes and costs are transferred at different places. The parties are well advised to identify as precisely as possible in the contract both the place of delivery, where the risk passes to the buyer, and the named place of destination to which the seller must contract for the carriage. If several carriers are used for the carriage to the agreed destination and the parties do not agree on a specific point of delivery, the default position is that risk passes when the goods have been delivered to the first carrier at a point entirely of the seller's choosing and over which the buyer has no control. Should the parties wish the risk to pass at a later stage (e.g., at an ocean port or airport), they need to specify this in their contract of sale.

The parties are also well advised to identify as precisely as possible the point within the agreed place of destination, as the costs to that point are for the account of the seller. The seller is advised to procure contracts of carriage that match this choice precisely. If the seller incurs costs under its contract of carriage related to unloading at the named place of destination, the seller is not entitled to recover such costs from the buyer unless otherwise agreed between the parties.

CPT requires the seller to clear the goods for export, where applicable. However, the seller has no obligation to clear the goods for import, pay any import duty or carry out any import customs formalities.

A THE SELLER'S OBLIGATIONS

A1 General obligations of the seller

The seller must provide the goods and the commercial invoice in conformity with the contract of sale and any other evidence of conformity that may be required by the contract.

Any document referred to in **A1–A10** may be an equivalent electronic record or procedure if agreed between the parties or customary.

A2 Licences, authorizations, security clearances and other formalities

Where applicable, the seller must obtain, at its own risk and expense, any export licence or other official authorization and carry out all customs formalities necessary for the export of the goods, and for their transport through any country prior to delivery.

A3 Contracts of carriage and insurance

a. Contract of carriage

The seller must contract or procure a contract for the carriage of the goods from the agreed point of delivery, if any, at the place of delivery to the named place of destination or, if agreed, any point at that place. The contract of carriage must be made on usual terms at the seller's expense and provide for carriage by the usual route and in a customary manner. If a specific point is not agreed or is not determined by practice, the seller may select the point of delivery and the point at the named place of destination that best suit its purpose.

b. Contract of insurance

The seller has no obligation to the buyer to make a contract of insurance. However, the seller must provide the buyer, at the buyer's request, risk, and expense (if any), with information that the buyer needs for obtaining insurance.

A4 Delivery

The seller must deliver the goods by handing them over to the carrier contracted in accordance with **A3** on the agreed date or within the agreed period.

B THE BUYER'S OBLIGATIONS

B1 General obligations of the buyer

The buyer must pay the price of the goods as provided in the contract of sale.

Any document referred to in **B1–B10** may be an equivalent electronic record or procedure if agreed between the parties or customary.

B2 Licences, authorizations, security clearances and other formalities

Where applicable, it is up to the buyer to obtain, at its own risk and expense, any import licence or other official authorization and carry out all customs formalities for the import of the goods and for their transport through any country.

B3 Contracts of carriage and insurance

a. Contract of carriage

The buyer has no obligation to the seller to make a contract of carriage.

b. Contract of insurance

The buyer has no obligation to the seller to make a contract of insurance. However, the buyer must provide the seller, upon request, with the necessary information for obtaining insurance.

B4 Taking delivery

The buyer must take delivery of the goods when they have been delivered as envisaged in **A4** and receive them from the carrier at the named place of destination.

A5 Transfer of risks

The seller bears all risks of loss of or damage to the goods until they have been delivered in accordance with **A4**, with the exception of loss or damage in the circumstances described in **B5**.

A6 Allocation of costs

The seller must pay

a. all costs relating to the goods until they have been delivered in accordance with **A4**, other than those payable by the buyer as envisaged in **B6**;

b. the freight and all other costs resulting from **A3 a**, including the costs of loading the goods and any charges for unloading at the place of destination that were for the seller's account under the contract of carriage; and

c. where applicable, the costs of customs formalities necessary for export, as well as all duties, taxes and other charges payable upon export, and the costs for their transport through any country that were for the seller's account under the contract of carriage.

A7 Notices to the buyer

The seller must notify the buyer that the goods have been delivered in accordance with **A4**.

The seller must give the buyer any notice needed in order to allow the buyer to take measures that are normally necessary to enable the buyer to take the goods.

B5 Transfer of risks

The buyer bears all risks of loss of or damage to the goods from the time they have been delivered as envisaged in **A4**.

If the buyer fails to give notice in accordance with **B7**, it must bear all risks of loss of or damage to the goods from the agreed date or the expiry date of the agreed period for delivery, provided that the goods have been clearly identified as the contract goods.

B6 Allocation of costs

The buyer must, subject to the provisions of **A3 a**, pay

a. all costs relating to the goods from the time they have been delivered as envisaged in **A4**, except, where applicable, the costs of customs formalities necessary for export, as well as all duties, taxes, and other charges payable upon export as referred to in **A6 c**;

b. all costs and charges relating to the goods while in transit until their arrival at the agreed place of destination, unless such costs and charges were for the seller's account under the contract of carriage;

c. unloading costs, unless such costs were for the seller's account under the contract of carriage;

d. any additional costs incurred if the buyer fails to give notice in accordance with **B7**, from the agreed date or the expiry date of the agreed period for dispatch, provided that the goods have been clearly identified as the contract goods; and

e. where applicable, all duties, taxes and other charges, as well as the costs of carrying out customs formalities payable upon import of the goods and the costs for their transport through any country, unless included within the cost of the contract of carriage.

B7 Notices to the seller

The buyer must, whenever it is entitled to determine the time for dispatching the goods and/or the named place of destination or the point of receiving the goods within that place, give the seller sufficient notice thereof.

A8 Delivery document

If customary or at the buyer's request, the seller must provide the buyer, at the seller's expense, with the usual transport document[s] for the transport contracted in accordance with **A3**.

This transport document must cover the contract goods and be dated within the period agreed for shipment. If agreed or customary, the document must also enable the buyer to claim the goods from the carrier at the named place of destination and enable the buyer to sell the goods in transit by the transfer of the document to a subsequent buyer or by notification to the carrier.

When such a transport document is issued in negotiable form and in several originals, a full set of originals must be presented to the buyer.

A9 Checking – packaging – marking

The seller must pay the costs of those checking operations (such as checking quality, measuring, weighing, counting) that are necessary for the purpose of delivering the goods in accordance with **A4**, as well as the costs of any pre-shipment inspection mandated by the authority of the country of export.

The seller must, at its own expense, package the goods, unless it is usual for the particular trade to transport the type of goods sold unpackaged. The seller may package the goods in the manner appropriate for their transport, unless the buyer has notified the seller of specific packaging requirements before the contract of sale is concluded. Packaging is to be marked appropriately.

A10 Assistance with information and related costs

The seller must, where applicable, in a timely manner, provide to or render assistance in obtaining for the buyer, at the buyer's request, risk and expense, any documents and information, including security-related information, that the buyer needs for the import of the goods and/or for their transport to the final destination.

The seller must reimburse the buyer for all costs and charges incurred by the buyer in providing or rendering assistance in obtaining documents and information as envisaged in **B10**.

B8 Proof of delivery

The buyer must accept the transport document provided as envisaged in **A8** if it is in conformity with the contract.

B9 Inspection of goods

The buyer must pay the costs of any mandatory pre-shipment inspection, except when such inspection is mandated by the authorities of the country of export.

B10 Assistance with information and related costs

The buyer must, in a timely manner, advise the seller of any security information requirements so that the seller may comply with **A10**.

The buyer must reimburse the seller for all costs and charges incurred by the seller in providing or rendering assistance in obtaining documents and information as envisaged in **A10**.

The buyer must, where applicable, in a timely manner, provide to or render assistance in obtaining for the seller, at the seller's request, risk and expense, any documents and information, including security-related information, that the seller needs for the transport and export of the goods and for their transport through any country.

CIP

CARRIAGE AND INSURANCE PAID TO

CIP *(insert named place of destination)* Incoterms® 2010

GUIDANCE NOTE

This rule may be used irrespective of the mode of transport selected and may also be used where more than one mode of transport is employed.

"Carriage and Insurance Paid to" means that the seller delivers the goods to the carrier or another person nominated by the seller at an agreed place (if any such place is agreed between the parties) and that the seller must contract for and pay the costs of carriage necessary to bring the goods to the named place of destination.

The seller also contracts for insurance cover against the buyer's risk of loss of or damage to the goods during the carriage. The buyer should note that under CIP the seller is required to obtain insurance only on minimum cover. Should the buyer wish to have more insurance protection, it will need either to agree as much expressly with the seller or to make its own extra insurance arrangements.

When CPT, CIP, CFR or CIF are used, the seller fulfils its obligation to deliver when it hands the goods over to the carrier and not when the goods reach the place of destination.

This rule has two critical points, because risk passes and costs are transferred at different places. The parties are well advised to identify as precisely as possible in the contract both the place of delivery, where the risk passes to the buyer, and the named place of destination to which the seller must contract for carriage. If several carriers are used for the carriage to the agreed destination and the parties do not agree on a specific point of delivery, the default position is that risk passes when the goods have been delivered to the first carrier at a point entirely of the seller's choosing and over which the buyer has no control. Should the parties wish the risk to pass at a later stage (e.g., at an ocean port or an airport), they need to specify this in their contract of sale.

The parties are also well advised to identify as precisely as possible the point within the agreed place of destination, as the costs to that point are for the account of the seller. The seller is advised to procure contracts of carriage that match this choice precisely. If the seller incurs costs under its contract of carriage related to unloading at the named place of destination, the seller is not entitled to recover such costs from the buyer unless otherwise agreed between the parties.

CIP requires the seller to clear the goods for export, where applicable. However, the seller has no obligation to clear the goods for import, pay any import duty or carry out any import customs formalities.

A THE SELLER'S OBLIGATIONS

A1 General obligations of the seller

The seller must provide the goods and the commercial invoice in conformity with the contract of sale and any other evidence of conformity that may be required by the contract.

Any document referred to in **A1–A10** may be an equivalent electronic record or procedure if agreed between the parties or customary.

A2 Licences, authorizations, security clearances and other formalities

Where applicable, the seller must obtain, at its own risk and expense, any export licence or other official authorization and carry out all customs formalities necessary for the export of the goods and for their transport through any country prior to delivery.

A3 Contracts of carriage and insurance

a. Contract of carriage

The seller must contract or procure a contract for the carriage of the goods from the agreed point of delivery, if any, at the place of delivery to the named place of destination or, if agreed, any point at that place. The contract of carriage must be made on usual terms at the seller's expense and provide for carriage by the usual route and in a customary manner. If a specific point is not agreed or is not determined by practice, the seller may select the point of delivery and the point at the named place of destination that best suit its purpose.

b. Contract of insurance

The seller must obtain at its own expense cargo insurance complying at least with the minimum cover as provided by Clauses (C) of the Institute Cargo Clauses (LMA/IUA) or any similar clauses. The insurance shall be contracted with underwriters or an insurance company of good repute and entitle the buyer, or any other person having an insurable interest in the goods, to claim directly from the insurer.

When required by the buyer, the seller shall, subject to the buyer providing any necessary information requested by the seller, provide at the buyer's expense any additional

B THE BUYER'S OBLIGATIONS

B1 General obligations of the buyer

The buyer must pay the price of the goods as provided in the contract of sale.

Any document referred to in **B1–B10** may be an equivalent electronic record or procedure if agreed between the parties or customary.

B2 Licences, authorizations, security clearances and other formalities

Where applicable, it is up to the buyer to obtain, at its own risk and expense, any import licence or other official authorization and carry out all customs formalities for the import of the goods and for their transport through any country.

B3 Contracts of carriage and insurance

a. Contract of carriage
   The buyer has no obligation to the seller to make a contract of carriage.

b. Contract of insurance
   The buyer has no obligation to the seller to make a contract of insurance. However, the buyer must provide the seller, upon request, with any information necessary for the seller to procure any additional insurance requested by the buyer as envisaged in **A3 b.**

cover, if procurable, such as cover as provided by Clauses (A) or (B) of the Institute Cargo Clauses (LMA/IUA) or any similar clauses, and/or cover complying with the Institute War Clauses and/or Institute Strikes Clauses (LMA/IUA) or any similar clauses.

The insurance shall cover, at a minimum, the price provided in the contract plus 10% (i.e., 110%) and shall be in the currency of the contract.

The insurance shall cover the goods from the point of delivery set out in **A4** and **A5** to at least the named place of destination.

The seller must provide the buyer with the insurance policy or other evidence of insurance cover.

Moreover, the seller must provide the buyer, at the buyer's request, risk, and expense (if any), with information that the buyer needs to procure any additional insurance.

A4 Delivery

The seller must deliver the goods by handing them over to the carrier contracted in accordance with **A3** on the agreed date or within the agreed period.

A5 Transfer of risks

The seller bears all risks of loss of or damage to the goods until they have been delivered in accordance with **A4**, with the exception of loss or damage in the circumstances described in **B5**.

A6 Allocation of costs

The seller must pay

a. all costs relating to the goods until they have been delivered in accordance with **A4**, other than those payable by the buyer as envisaged in **B6**;

B4 Taking delivery

The buyer must take delivery of the goods when they have been delivered as envisaged in **A4** and receive them from the carrier at the named place of destination.

B5 Transfer of risks

The buyer bears all risks of loss of or damage to the goods from the time they have been delivered as envisaged in **A4**.

If the buyer fails to give notice in accordance with **B7**, it must bear all risks of loss of or damage to the goods from the agreed date or the expiry date of the agreed period for delivery, provided that the goods have been clearly identified as the contract goods.

B6 Allocation of costs

The buyer must, subject to the provisions of **A3 a**, pay

a. all costs relating to the goods from the time they have been delivered as envisaged in **A4**, except, where applicable, the costs of customs formalities necessary for export, as well as all duties, taxes and other charges payable upon export as referred to in **A6 d**;

b. the freight and all other costs resulting from **A3 a**, including the costs of loading the goods and any charges for unloading at the place of destination that were for the seller's account under the contract of carriage;

c. the costs of insurance resulting from **A3 b**; and

d. where applicable, the costs of customs formalities necessary for export, as well as all duties, taxes and other charges payable upon export, and the costs for their transport through any country that were for the seller's account under the contract of carriage.

A7 Notices to the buyer

The seller must notify the buyer that the goods have been delivered in accordance with **A4**.

The seller must give the buyer any notice needed in order to allow the buyer to take measures that are normally necessary to enable the buyer to take the goods.

A8 Delivery document

If customary or at the buyer's request, the seller must provide the buyer, at the seller's expense, with the usual transport document[s] for the transport contracted in accordance with **A3**.

This transport document must cover the contract goods and be dated within the period agreed for shipment. If agreed or customary, the document must also enable the buyer to claim the goods from the carrier at the named place of destination and enable the buyer to sell the goods in transit by the transfer of the document to a subsequent buyer or by notification to the carrier.

b. all costs and charges relating to the goods while in transit until their arrival at the agreed place of destination, unless such costs and charges were for the seller's account under the contract of carriage;

c. unloading costs, unless such costs were for the seller's account under the contract of carriage;

d. any additional costs incurred if it fails to give notice in accordance with **B7**, from the agreed date or the expiry date of the agreed period for dispatch, provided that the goods have been clearly identified as the contract goods;

e. where applicable, all duties, taxes and other charges as well as the costs of carrying out customs formalities payable upon import of the goods and the costs for their transport through any country, unless included within the cost of the contract of carriage; and

f. the costs of any additional insurance procured at the buyer's request under **A3** and **B3**.

B7 Notices to the seller

The buyer must, whenever it is entitled to determine the time for dispatching the goods and/or the named place of destination or the point of receiving the goods within that place, give the seller sufficient notice thereof.

B8 Proof of delivery

The buyer must accept the transport document provided as envisaged in **A8** if it is in conformity with the contract.

When such a transport document is issued in negotiable form and in several originals, a full set of originals must be presented to the buyer.

A9 Checking – packaging – marking

The seller must pay the costs of those checking operations (such as checking quality, measuring, weighing, counting) that are necessary for the purpose of delivering the goods in accordance with **A4** as well as the costs of any pre-shipment inspection mandated by the authority of the country of export.

The seller must, at its own expense, package the goods, unless it is usual for the particular trade to transport the type of goods sold unpackaged. The seller may package the goods in the manner appropriate for their transport, unless the buyer has notified the seller of specific packaging requirements before the contract of sale is concluded. Packaging is to be marked appropriately.

A10 Assistance with information and related costs

The seller must, where applicable, in a timely manner, provide to or render assistance in obtaining for the buyer, at the buyer's request, risk and expense, any documents and information, including security-related information, that the buyer needs for the import of the goods and/or for their transport to the final destination.

The seller must reimburse the buyer for all costs and charges incurred by the buyer in providing or rendering assistance in obtaining documents and information as envisaged in **B10**.

B9 Inspection of goods

The buyer must pay the costs of any mandatory pre-shipment inspection, except when such inspection is mandated by the authorities of the country of export.

B10 Assistance with information and related costs

The buyer must, in a timely manner, advise the seller of any security information requirements so that the seller may comply with **A10**.

The buyer must reimburse the seller for all costs and charges incurred by the seller in providing or rendering assistance in obtaining documents and information as envisaged in **A10**.

The buyer must, where applicable, in a timely manner, provide to or render assistance in obtaining for the seller, at the seller's request, risk and expense, any documents and information, including security-related information, that the seller needs for the transport and export of the goods and for their transport through any country.

DAT

DELIVERED AT TERMINAL

DAT *(insert named terminal at port or place of destination)* Incoterms® 2010

GUIDANCE NOTE

This rule may be used irrespective of the mode of transport selected and may also be used where more than one mode of transport is employed.

"Delivered at Terminal" means that the seller delivers when the goods, once unloaded from the arriving means of transport, are placed at the disposal of the buyer at a named terminal at the named port or place of destination. "Terminal" includes any place, whether covered or not, such as a quay, warehouse, container yard or road, rail or air cargo terminal. The seller bears all risks involved in bringing the goods to and unloading them at the terminal at the named port or place of destination.

The parties are well advised to specify as clearly as possible the terminal and, if possible, a specific point within the terminal at the agreed port or place of destination, as the risks to that point are for the account of the seller. The seller is advised to procure a contract of carriage that matches this choice precisely.

Moreover, if the parties intend the seller to bear the risks and costs involved in transporting and handling the goods from the terminal to another place, then the DAP or DDP rules should be used.

DAT requires the seller to clear the goods for export, where applicable. However, the seller has no obligation to clear the goods for import, pay any import duty or carry out any import customs formalities.

A THE SELLER'S OBLIGATIONS

A1 General obligations of the seller

The seller must provide the goods and the commercial invoice in conformity with the contract of sale and any other evidence of conformity that may be required by the contract.

Any document referred to in **A1–A10** may be an equivalent electronic record or procedure if agreed between the parties or customary.

A2 Licences, authorizations, security clearances and other formalities

Where applicable, the seller must obtain, at its own risk and expense, any export licence and other official authorization and carry out all customs formalities necessary for the export of the goods and for their transport through any country prior to delivery.

A3 Contracts of carriage and insurance

a. Contract of carriage

The seller must contract at its own expense for the carriage of the goods to the named terminal at the agreed port or place of destination. If a specific terminal is not agreed or is not determined by practice, the seller may select the terminal at the agreed port or place of destination that best suits its purpose.

b. Contract of insurance

The seller has no obligation to the buyer to make a contract of insurance. However, the seller must provide the buyer, at the buyer's request, risk, and expense (if any), with information that the buyer needs for obtaining insurance.

A4 Delivery

The seller must unload the goods from the arriving means of transport and must then deliver them by placing them at the disposal of the buyer at the named terminal referred to in **A3 a** at the port or place of destination on the agreed date or within the agreed period.

B THE BUYER'S OBLIGATIONS

B1 General obligations of the buyer

The buyer must pay the price of the goods as provided in the contract of sale.

Any document referred to in **B1–B10** may be an equivalent electronic record or procedure if agreed between the parties or customary.

B2 Licences, authorizations, security clearances and other formalities

Where applicable, the buyer must obtain, at its own risk and expense, any import licence or other official authorization and carry out all customs formalities for the import of the goods.

B3 Contracts of carriage and insurance

a. Contract of carriage
The buyer has no obligation to the seller to make a contract of carriage.

b. Contract of insurance
The buyer has no obligation to the seller to make a contract of insurance. However, the buyer must provide the seller, upon request, with the necessary information for obtaining insurance.

B4 Taking delivery

The buyer must take delivery of the goods when they have been delivered as envisaged in **A4**.

A5 Transfer of risks

The seller bears all risks of loss of or damage to the goods until they have been delivered in accordance with **A4** with the exception of loss or damage in the circumstances described in **B5**.

A6 Allocation of costs

The seller must pay

a. in addition to costs resulting from **A3 a**, all costs relating to the goods until they have been delivered in accordance with **A4**, other than those payable by the buyer as envisaged in **B6**; and

b. where applicable, the costs of customs formalities necessary for export as well as all duties, taxes and other charges payable upon export and the costs for their transport through any country, prior to delivery in accordance with **A4**.

A7 Notices to the buyer

The seller must give the buyer any notice needed in order to allow the buyer to take measures that are normally necessary to enable the buyer to take delivery of the goods.

A8 Delivery document

The seller must provide the buyer, at the seller's expense, with a document enabling the buyer to take delivery of the goods as envisaged in **A4/B4**.

B5 Transfer of risks

The buyer bears all risks of loss of or damage to the goods from the time they have been delivered as envisaged in A4.

If

a. the buyer fails to fulfil its obligations in accordance with B2, then it bears all resulting risks of loss of or damage to the goods; or

b. the buyer fails to give notice in accordance with B7, then it bears all risks of loss of or damage to the goods from the agreed date or the expiry date of the agreed period for delivery,

provided that the goods have been clearly identified as the contract goods.

B6 Allocation of costs

The buyer must pay

a. all costs relating to the goods from the time they have been delivered as envisaged in A4;

b. any additional costs incurred by the seller if the buyer fails to fulfil its obligations in accordance with B2, or to give notice in accordance with B7, provided that the goods have been clearly identified as the contract goods; and

c. where applicable, the costs of customs formalities as well as all duties, taxes and other charges payable upon import of the goods.

B7 Notices to the seller

The buyer must, whenever it is entitled to determine the time within an agreed period and/or the point of taking delivery at the named terminal, give the seller sufficient notice thereof.

B8 Proof of delivery

The buyer must accept the delivery document provided as envisaged in A8.

A9 Checking – packaging – marking

The seller must pay the costs of those checking operations (such as checking quality, measuring, weighing, counting) that are necessary for the purpose of delivering the goods in accordance with **A4**, as well as the costs of any pre-shipment inspection mandated by the authority of the country of export.

The seller must, at its own expense, package the goods, unless it is usual for the particular trade to transport the type of goods sold unpackaged. The seller may package the goods in the manner appropriate for their transport, unless the buyer has notified the seller of specific packaging requirements before the contract of sale is concluded. Packaging is to be marked appropriately.

A10 Assistance with information and related costs

The seller must, where applicable, in a timely manner, provide to or render assistance in obtaining for the buyer, at the buyer's request, risk and expense, any documents and information, including security-related information, that the buyer needs for the import of the goods and/or for their transport to the final destination.

The seller must reimburse the buyer for all costs and charges incurred by the buyer in providing or rendering assistance in obtaining documents and information as envisaged in **B10**.

B9 Inspection of goods

The buyer must pay the costs of any mandatory pre-shipment inspection, except when such inspection is mandated by the authorities of the country of export.

B10 Assistance with information and related costs

The buyer must, in a timely manner, advise the seller of any security information requirements so that the seller may comply with **A10**.

The buyer must reimburse the seller for all costs and charges incurred by the seller in providing or rendering assistance in obtaining documents and information as envisaged in **A10**.

The buyer must, where applicable, in a timely manner, provide to or render assistance in obtaining for the seller, at the seller's request, risk and expense, any documents and information, including security-related information, that the seller needs for the transport and export of the goods and for their transport through any country.

DAP

DELIVERED AT PLACE

DAP *(insert named place of destination)* Incoterms® 2010

GUIDANCE NOTE

This rule may be used irrespective of the mode of transport selected and may also be used where more than one mode of transport is employed.

"Delivered at Place" means that the seller delivers when the goods are placed at the disposal of the buyer on the arriving means of transport ready for unloading at the named place of destination. The seller bears all risks involved in bringing the goods to the named place.

The parties are well advised to specify as clearly as possible the point within the agreed place of destination, as the risks to that point are for the account of the seller. The seller is advised to procure contracts of carriage that match this choice precisely. If the seller incurs costs under its contract of carriage related to unloading at the place of destination, the seller is not entitled to recover such costs from the buyer unless otherwise agreed between the parties.

DAP requires the seller to clear the goods for export, where applicable. However, the seller has no obligation to clear the goods for import, pay any import duty or carry out any import customs formalities. If the parties wish the seller to clear the goods for import, pay any import duty and carry out any import customs formalities, the DDP term should be used.

A THE SELLER'S OBLIGATIONS

A1 General obligations of the seller

The seller must provide the goods and the commercial invoice in conformity with the contract of sale and any other evidence of conformity that may be required by the contract.

Any document referred to in **A1–A10** may be an equivalent electronic record or procedure if agreed between the parties or customary.

A2 Licences, authorizations, security clearances and other formalities

Where applicable, the seller must obtain, at its own risk and expense, any export licence and other official authorization and carry out all customs formalities necessary for the export of the goods and for their transport through any country prior to delivery.

A3 Contracts of carriage and insurance

a. Contract of carriage

The seller must contract at its own expense for the carriage of the goods to the named place of destination or to the agreed point, if any, at the named place of destination. If a specific point is not agreed or is not determined by practice, the seller may select the point at the named place of destination that best suits its purpose.

b. Contract of insurance

The seller has no obligation to the buyer to make a contract of insurance. However, the seller must provide the buyer, at the buyer's request, risk, and expense (if any), with information that the buyer needs for obtaining insurance.

A4 Delivery

The seller must deliver the goods by placing them at the disposal of the buyer on the arriving means of transport ready for unloading at the agreed point, if any, at the named place of destination on the agreed date or within the agreed period.

B THE BUYER'S OBLIGATIONS

B1 General obligations of the buyer

The buyer must pay the price of the goods as provided in the contract of sale.

Any document referred to in **B1–B10** may be an equivalent electronic record or procedure if agreed between the parties or customary.

B2 Licences, authorizations, security clearances and other formalities

Where applicable, the buyer must obtain, at its own risk and expense, any import licence or other official authorization and carry out all customs formalities for the import of the goods.

B3 Contracts of carriage and insurance

a. Contract of carriage
   The buyer has no obligation to the seller to make a contract of carriage.

b. Contract of insurance
   The buyer has no obligation to the seller to make a contract of insurance. However, the buyer must provide the seller, upon request, with the necessary information for obtaining insurance.

B4 Taking delivery

The buyer must take delivery of the goods when they have been delivered as envisaged in **A4**.

A5 Transfer of risks

The seller bears all risks of loss of or damage to the goods until they have been delivered in accordance with **A4**, with the exception of loss or damage in the circumstances described in **B5**.

A6 Allocation of costs

The seller must pay

a. in addition to costs resulting from **A3 a**, all costs relating to the goods until they have been delivered in accordance with **A4**, other than those payable by the buyer as envisaged in **B6**;

b. any charges for unloading at the place of destination that were for the seller's account under the contract of carriage; and

c. where applicable, the costs of customs formalities necessary for export as well as all duties, taxes and other charges payable upon export and the costs for their transport through any country, prior to delivery in accordance with **A4**.

A7 Notices to the buyer

The seller must give the buyer any notice needed in order to allow the buyer to take measures that are normally necessary to enable the buyer to take delivery of the goods.

B5 Transfer of risks

The buyer bears all risks of loss of or damage to the goods from the time they have been delivered as envisaged in **A4**.

If

a. the buyer fails to fulfil its obligations in accordance with **B2**, then it bears all resulting risks of loss of or damage to the goods; or

b. the buyer fails to give notice in accordance with **B7**, then it bears all risks of loss of or damage to the goods from the agreed date or the expiry date of the agreed period for delivery,

provided that the goods have been clearly identified as the contract goods.

B6 Allocation of costs

The buyer must pay

a. all costs relating to the goods from the time they have been delivered as envisaged in **A4**;

b. all costs of unloading necessary to take delivery of the goods from the arriving means of transport at the named place of destination, unless such costs were for the seller's account under the contract of carriage;

c. any additional costs incurred by the seller if the buyer fails to fulfil its obligations in accordance with **B2** or to give notice in accordance with **B7**, provided that the goods have been clearly identified as the contract goods; and

d. where applicable, the costs of customs formalities, as well as all duties, taxes and other charges payable upon import of the goods.

B7 Notices to the seller

The buyer must, whenever it is entitled to determine the time within an agreed period and/or the point of taking delivery within the named place of destination, give the seller sufficient notice thereof.

A8 Delivery document

The seller must provide the buyer, at the seller's expense, with a document enabling the buyer to take delivery of the goods as envisaged in **A4/B4**.

A9 Checking – packaging – marking

The seller must pay the costs of those checking operations (such as checking quality, measuring, weighing, counting) that are necessary for the purpose of delivering the goods in accordance with **A4**, as well as the costs of any pre-shipment inspection mandated by the authority of the country of export.

The seller must, at its own expense, package the goods, unless it is usual for the particular trade to transport the type of goods sold unpackaged. The seller may package the goods in the manner appropriate for their transport, unless the buyer has notified the seller of specific packaging requirements before the contract of sale is concluded. Packaging is to be marked appropriately.

A10 Assistance with information and related costs

The seller must, where applicable, in a timely manner, provide to or render assistance in obtaining for the buyer, at the buyer's request, risk and expense, any documents and information, including security-related information, that the buyer needs for the import of the goods and/or for their transport to the final destination.

The seller must reimburse the buyer for all costs and charges incurred by the buyer in providing or rendering assistance in obtaining documents and information as envisaged in **B10**.

B8 Proof of delivery

The buyer must accept the delivery document provided as envisaged in A8.

B9 Inspection of goods

The buyer must pay the costs of any mandatory pre-shipment inspection, except when such inspection is mandated by the authorities of the country of export.

B10 Assistance with information and related costs

The buyer must, in a timely manner, advise the seller of any security information requirements so that the seller may comply with A10.

The buyer must reimburse the seller for all costs and charges incurred by the seller in providing or rendering assistance in obtaining documents and information as envisaged in A10.

The buyer must, where applicable, in a timely manner, provide to or render assistance in obtaining for the seller, at the seller's request, risk and expense, any documents and information, including security-related information, that the seller needs for the transport and export of the goods and for their transport through any country.

DDP
DELIVERED DUTY PAID

DDP *(insert named place of destination)* Incoterms® 2010

GUIDANCE NOTE

This rule may be used irrespective of the mode of transport selected and may also be used where more than one mode of transport is employed.

"Delivered Duty Paid" means that the seller delivers the goods when the goods are placed at the disposal of the buyer, cleared for import on the arriving means of transport ready for unloading at the named place of destination. The seller bears all the costs and risks involved in bringing the goods to the place of destination and has an obligation to clear the goods not only for export but also for import, to pay any duty for both export and import and to carry out all customs formalities.

DDP represents the maximum obligation for the seller.

The parties are well advised to specify as clearly as possible the point within the agreed place of destination, as the costs and risks to that point are for the account of the seller. The seller is advised to procure contracts of carriage that match this choice precisely. If the seller incurs costs under its contract of carriage related to unloading at the place of destination, the seller is not entitled to recover such costs from the buyer unless otherwise agreed between the parties.

The parties are well advised not to use DDP if the seller is unable directly or indirectly to obtain import clearance.

If the parties wish the buyer to bear all risks and costs of import clearance, the DAP rule should be used.

Any VAT or other taxes payable upon import are for the seller's account unless expressly agreed otherwise in the sales contract.

A THE SELLER'S OBLIGATIONS

A1 General obligations of the seller

The seller must provide the goods and the commercial invoice in conformity with the contract of sale and any other evidence of conformity that may be required by the contract.

Any document referred to in **A1–A10** may be an equivalent electronic record or procedure if agreed between the parties or customary.

A2 Licences, authorizations, security clearances and other formalities

Where applicable, the seller must obtain, at its own risk and expense, any export and import licence and other official authorization and carry out all customs formalities necessary for the export of the goods, for their transport through any country and for their import.

A3 Contracts of carriage and insurance

a. Contract of carriage

The seller must contract at its own expense for the carriage of the goods to the named place of destination or to the agreed point, if any, at the named place of destination. If a specific point is not agreed or is not determined by practice, the seller may select the point at the named place of destination that best suits its purpose.

b. Contract of insurance

The seller has no obligation to the buyer to make a contract of insurance. However, the seller must provide the buyer, at the buyer's request, risk, and expense (if any), with information that the buyer needs for obtaining insurance.

A4 Delivery

The seller must deliver the goods by placing them at the disposal of the buyer on the arriving means of transport ready for unloading at the agreed point, if any, at the named place of destination on the agreed date or within the agreed period.

B THE BUYER'S OBLIGATIONS

B1 General obligations of the buyer

The buyer must pay the price of the goods as provided in the contract of sale.

Any document referred to in **B1–B10** may be an equivalent electronic record or procedure if agreed between the parties or customary.

B2 Licences, authorizations, security clearances and other formalities

Where applicable, the buyer must provide assistance to the seller, at the seller's request, risk and expense, in obtaining any import licence or other official authorization for the import of the goods.

B3 Contracts of carriage and insurance

a. Contract of carriage
The buyer has no obligation to the seller to make a contract of carriage.

b. Contract of insurance
The buyer has no obligation to the seller to make a contract of insurance. However, the buyer must provide the seller, upon request, with the necessary information for obtaining insurance.

B4 Taking delivery

The buyer must take delivery of the goods when they have been delivered as envisaged in **A4**.

A5 **Transfer of risks**

The seller bears all risks of loss of or damage to the goods until they have been delivered in accordance with **A4**, with the exception of loss or damage in the circumstances described in **B5**.

A6 **Allocation of costs**

The seller must pay

a. in addition to costs resulting from **A3 a**, all costs relating to the goods until they have been delivered in accordance with **A4**, other than those payable by the buyer as envisaged in **B6**;

b. any charges for unloading at the place of destination that were for the seller's account under the contract of carriage; and

c. where applicable, the costs of customs formalities necessary for export and import as well as all duties, taxes and other charges payable upon export and import of the goods, and the costs for their transport through any country prior to delivery in accordance with **A4**.

A7 **Notices to the buyer**

The seller must give the buyer any notice needed in order to allow the buyer to take measures that are normally necessary to enable the buyer to take delivery of the goods.

A8 **Delivery document**

The seller must provide the buyer, at the seller's expense, with a document enabling the buyer to take delivery of the goods as envisaged in **A4/B4**.

B5 Transfer of risks

The buyer bears all risks of loss of or damage to the goods from the time they have been delivered as envisaged in A4.

If

a. the buyer fails to fulfil its obligations in accordance with B2, then it bears all resulting risks of loss of or damage to the goods; or

b. the buyer fails to give notice in accordance with B7, then it bears all risks of loss of or damage to the goods from the agreed date or the expiry date of the agreed period for delivery,

provided that the goods have been clearly identified as the contract goods.

B6 Allocation of costs

The buyer must pay

a. all costs relating to the goods from the time they have been delivered as envisaged in A4;

b. all costs of unloading necessary to take delivery of the goods from the arriving means of transport at the named place of destination, unless such costs were for the seller's account under the contract of carriage; and

c. any additional costs incurred if it fails to fulfil its obligations in accordance with B2 or to give notice in accordance with B7, provided that the goods have been clearly identified as the contract goods.

B7 Notices to the seller

The buyer must, whenever it is entitled to determine the time within an agreed period and/or the point of taking delivery within the named place of destination, give the seller sufficient notice thereof.

B8 Proof of delivery

The buyer must accept the proof of delivery provided as envisaged in A8.

A9 Checking – packaging – marking

The seller must pay the costs of those checking operations (such as checking quality, measuring, weighing, counting) that are necessary for the purpose of delivering the goods in accordance with **A4**, as well as the costs of any pre-shipment inspection mandated by the authority of the country of export or of import.

The seller must, at its own expense, package the goods, unless it is usual for the particular trade to transport the type of goods sold unpackaged. The seller may package the goods in the manner appropriate for their transport, unless the buyer has notified the seller of specific packaging requirements before the contract of sale is concluded. Packaging is to be marked appropriately.

A10 Assistance with information and related costs

The seller must, where applicable, in a timely manner, provide to or render assistance in obtaining for the buyer, at the buyer's request, risk and expense, any documents and information, including security-related information, that the buyer needs for the transport of the goods to the final destination, where applicable, from the named place of destination.

The seller must reimburse the buyer for all costs and charges incurred by the buyer in providing or rendering assistance in obtaining documents and information as envisaged in **B10**.

B9 Inspection of goods

The buyer has no obligation to the seller to pay the costs of any mandatory pre-shipment inspection mandated by the authority of the country of export or of import.

B10 Assistance with information and related costs

The buyer must, in a timely manner, advise the seller of any security information requirements so that the seller may comply with **A10**.

The buyer must reimburse the seller for all costs and charges incurred by the seller in providing or rendering assistance in obtaining documents and information as envisaged in **A10**.

The buyer must, where applicable, in a timely manner, provide to or render assistance in obtaining for the seller, at the seller's request, risk and expense, any documents and information, including security-related information, that the seller needs for the transport, export and import of the goods and for their transport through any country.

RULES FOR SEA AND INLAND WATERWAY TRANSPORT

FAS
FREE ALONGSIDE SHIP

FAS *(insert named port of shipment)* Incoterms® 2010

GUIDANCE NOTE

This rule is to be used only for sea or inland waterway transport.

"Free Alongside Ship" means that the seller delivers when the goods are placed alongside the vessel (e.g., on a quay or a barge) nominated by the buyer at the named port of shipment. The risk of loss of or damage to the goods passes when the goods are alongside the ship, and the buyer bears all costs from that moment onwards.

The parties are well advised to specify as clearly as possible the loading point at the named port of shipment, as the costs and risks to that point are for the account of the seller and these costs and associated handling charges may vary according to the practice of the port.

The seller is required either to deliver the goods alongside the ship or to procure goods already so delivered for shipment. The reference to "procure" here caters for multiple sales down a chain ('string sales'), particularly common in the commodity trades.

Where the goods are in containers, it is typical for the seller to hand the goods over to the carrier at a terminal and not alongside the vessel. In such situations, the FAS rule would be inappropriate, and the FCA rule should be used.

FAS requires the seller to clear the goods for export, where applicable. However, the seller has no obligation to clear the goods for import, pay any import duty or carry out any import customs formalities.

A THE SELLER'S OBLIGATIONS

A1 General obligations of the seller

The seller must provide the goods and the commercial invoice in conformity with the contract of sale and any other evidence of conformity that may be required by the contract.

Any document referred to in **A1–A10** may be an equivalent electronic record or procedure if agreed between the parties or customary.

A2 Licences, authorizations, security clearances and other formalities

Where applicable, the seller must obtain, at its own risk and expense, any export licence or other official authorization and carry out all customs formalities necessary for the export of the goods.

A3 Contracts of carriage and insurance

a. Contract of carriage
The seller has no obligation to the buyer to make a contract of carriage. However, if requested by the buyer or if it is commercial practice and the buyer does not give an instruction to the contrary in due time, the seller may contract for carriage on usual terms at the buyer's risk and expense. In either case, the seller may decline to make the contract of carriage and, if it does, shall promptly notify the buyer.

b. Contract of insurance
The seller has no obligation to the buyer to make a contract of insurance. However, the seller must provide the buyer, at the buyer's request, risk, and expense (if any), with information that the buyer needs for obtaining insurance.

A4 Delivery

The seller must deliver the goods either by placing them alongside the ship nominated by the buyer at the loading point, if any, indicated by the buyer at the named port of shipment or by procuring the goods so delivered. In either case, the seller must deliver the goods on the agreed date or within the agreed period and in the manner customary at the port.

If no specific loading point has been indicated by the buyer, the seller may select the point within the named port of

B THE BUYER'S OBLIGATIONS

B1 General obligations of the buyer

The buyer must pay the price of the goods as provided in the contract of sale.

Any document referred to in **B1–B10** may be an equivalent electronic record or procedure if agreed between the parties or customary.

B2 Licences, authorizations, security clearances and other formalities

Where applicable, it is up to the buyer to obtain, at its own risk and expense, any import licence or other official authorization and carry out all customs formalities for the import of the goods and for their transport through any country.

B3 Contracts of carriage and insurance

a. Contract of carriage

The buyer must contract, at its own expense for the carriage of the goods from the named port of shipment, except where the contract of carriage is made by the seller as provided for in **A3 a**.

b. Contract of insurance

The buyer has no obligation to the seller to make a contract of insurance.

B4 Taking delivery

The buyer must take delivery of the goods when they have been delivered as envisaged in **A4**.

shipment that best suits its purpose. If the parties have agreed that delivery should take place within a period, the buyer has the option to choose the date within that period.

A5 Transfer of risks

The seller bears all risks of loss of or damage to the goods until they have been delivered in accordance with **A4** with the exception of loss or damage in the circumstances described in **B5**.

A6 Allocation of costs

The seller must pay

a. all costs relating to the goods until they have been delivered in accordance with **A4**, other than those payable by the buyer as envisaged in **B6**; and

b. where applicable, the costs of customs formalities necessary for export as well as all duties, taxes and other charges payable upon export.

B5 Transfer of risks

The buyer bears all risks of loss of or damage to the goods from the time they have been delivered as envisaged in **A4**.

If

a. the buyer fails to give notice in accordance with **B7**; or

b. the vessel nominated by the buyer fails to arrive on time, or fails to take the goods or closes for cargo earlier than the time notified in accordance with **B7**;

then the buyer bears all risks of loss of or damage to the goods from the agreed date or the expiry date of the agreed period for delivery, provided that the goods have been clearly identified as the contract goods.

B6 Allocation of costs

The buyer must pay

a. all costs relating to the goods from the time they have been delivered as envisaged in **A4**, except, where applicable, the costs of customs formalities necessary for export as well as all duties, taxes, and other charges payable upon export as referred to in **A6 b**;

b. any additional costs incurred, either because:
   i. the buyer has failed to give appropriate notice in accordance with **B7**, or
   ii. the vessel nominated by the buyer fails to arrive on time, is unable to take the goods, or closes for cargo earlier than the time notified in accordance with **B7**,

   provided that the goods have been clearly identified as the contract goods; and

c. where applicable, all duties, taxes and other charges, as well as the costs of carrying out customs formalities payable upon import of the goods and the costs for their transport through any country.

A7 Notices to the buyer

The seller must, at the buyer's risk and expense, give the buyer sufficient notice either that the goods have been delivered in accordance with **A4** or that the vessel has failed to take the goods within the time agreed.

A8 Delivery document

The seller must provide the buyer, at the seller's expense, with the usual proof that the goods have been delivered in accordance with **A4**.

Unless such proof is a transport document, the seller must provide assistance to the buyer, at the buyer's request, risk and expense, in obtaining a transport document.

A9 Checking – packaging – marking

The seller must pay the costs of those checking operations (such as checking quality, measuring, weighing, counting) that are necessary for the purpose of delivering the goods in accordance with **A4**, as well as the costs of any pre-shipment inspection mandated by the authority of the country of export.

The seller must, at its own expense, package the goods, unless it is usual for the particular trade to transport the type of goods sold unpackaged. The seller may package the goods in the manner appropriate for their transport, unless the buyer has notified the seller of specific packaging requirements before the contract of sale is concluded. Packaging is to be marked appropriately.

A10 Assistance with information and related costs

The seller must, where applicable, in a timely manner, provide to or render assistance in obtaining for the buyer, at the buyer's request, risk and expense, any documents and information, including security-related information, that the buyer needs for the import of the goods and/or for their transport to the final destination.

The seller must reimburse the buyer for all costs and charges incurred by the buyer in providing or rendering assistance in obtaining documents and information as envisaged in **B10**.

B7 Notices to the seller

The buyer must give the seller sufficient notice of the vessel name, loading point and, where necessary, the selected delivery time within the agreed period.

B8 Proof of delivery

The buyer must accept the proof of delivery provided as envisaged in **A8**.

B9 Inspection of goods

The buyer must pay the costs of any mandatory pre-shipment inspection, except when such inspection is mandated by the authorities of the country of export.

B10 Assistance with information and related costs

The buyer must, in a timely manner, advise the seller of any security information requirements so that the seller may comply with **A10**.

The buyer must reimburse the seller for all costs and charges incurred by the seller in providing or rendering assistance in obtaining documents and information as envisaged in **A10**.

The buyer must, where applicable, in a timely manner, provide to or render assistance in obtaining for the seller, at the seller's request, risk and expense, any documents and information, including security-related information, that the seller needs for the transport and export of the goods and for their transport through any country.

FOB
FREE ON BOARD

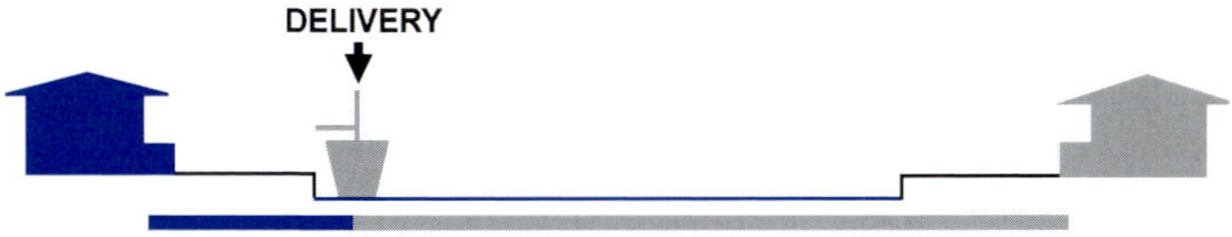

FOB *(insert named port of shipment)* Incoterms® 2010

GUIDANCE NOTE

This rule is to be used only for sea or inland waterway transport.

"Free on Board" means that the seller delivers the goods on board the vessel nominated by the buyer at the named port of shipment or procures the goods already so delivered. The risk of loss of or damage to the goods passes when the goods are on board the vessel, and the buyer bears all costs from that moment onwards.

The seller is required either to deliver the goods on board the vessel or to procure goods already so delivered for shipment. The reference to "procure" here caters for multiple sales down a chain ('string sales'), particularly common in the commodity trades.

FOB may not be appropriate where goods are handed over to the carrier before they are on board the vessel, for example goods in containers, which are typically delivered at a terminal. In such situations, the FCA rule should be used.

FOB requires the seller to clear the goods for export, where applicable. However, the seller has no obligation to clear the goods for import, pay any import duty or carry out any import customs formalities.

A THE SELLER'S OBLIGATIONS

A1 General obligations of the seller

The seller must provide the goods and the commercial invoice in conformity with the contract of sale and any other evidence of conformity that may be required by the contract.

Any document referred to in **A1–A10** may be an equivalent electronic record or procedure if agreed between the parties or customary.

A2 Licences, authorizations, security clearances and other formalities

Where applicable, the seller must obtain, at its own risk and expense, any export licence or other official authorization and carry out all customs formalities necessary for the export of the goods.

A3 Contracts of carriage and insurance

a. Contract of carriage

The seller has no obligation to the buyer to make a contract of carriage. However, if requested by the buyer or if it is commercial practice and the buyer does not give an instruction to the contrary in due time, the seller may contract for carriage on usual terms at the buyer's risk and expense. In either case, the seller may decline to make the contract of carriage and, if it does, shall promptly notify the buyer.

b. Contract of insurance

The seller has no obligation to the buyer to make a contract of insurance. However, the seller must provide the buyer, at the buyer's request, risk, and expense (if any), with information that the buyer needs for obtaining insurance.

B THE BUYER'S OBLIGATIONS

B1 General obligations of the buyer

The buyer must pay the price of the goods as provided in the contract of sale.

Any document referred to in **B1–B10** may be an equivalent electronic record or procedure if agreed between the parties or customary.

B2 Licences, authorizations, security clearances and other formalities

Where applicable, it is up to the buyer to obtain, at its own risk and expense, any import licence or other official authorization and carry out all customs formalities for the import of the goods and for their transport through any country.

B3 Contracts of carriage and insurance

a. Contract of carriage
   The buyer must contract, at its own expense for the carriage of the goods from the named port of shipment, except where the contract of carriage is made by the seller as provided for in **A3 a**.

b. Contract of insurance
   The buyer has no obligation to the seller to make a contract of insurance.

A4 Delivery

The seller must deliver the goods either by placing them on board the vessel nominated by the buyer at the loading point, if any, indicated by the buyer at the named port of shipment or by procuring the goods so delivered. In either case, the seller must deliver the goods on the agreed date or within the agreed period and in the manner customary at the port.

If no specific loading point has been indicated by the buyer, the seller may select the point within the named port of shipment that best suits its purpose.

A5 Transfer of risks

The seller bears all risks of loss of or damage to the goods until they have been delivered in accordance with **A4** with the exception of loss or damage in the circumstances described in **B5**.

B4 Taking delivery

The buyer must take delivery of the goods when they have been delivered as envisaged in **A4**.

B5 Transfer of risks

The buyer bears all risks of loss of or damage to the goods from the time they have been delivered as envisaged in **A4**.

If

a. the buyer fails to notify the nomination of a vessel in accordance with **B7**; or

b. the vessel nominated by the buyer fails to arrive on time to enable the seller to comply with **A4**, is unable to take the goods, or closes for cargo earlier than the time notified in accordance with **B7**;

then, the buyer bears all risks of loss of or damage to the goods:

i. from the agreed date, or in the absence of an agreed date,
ii. from the date notified by the seller under **A7** within the agreed period, or, if no such date has been notified,
iii. from the expiry date of any agreed period for delivery,

provided that the goods have been clearly identified as the contract goods.

A6 Allocation of costs

The seller must pay

a. all costs relating to the goods until they have been delivered in accordance with A4, other than those payable by the buyer as envisaged in B6; and

b. where applicable, the costs of customs formalities necessary for export, as well as all duties, taxes and other charges payable upon export.

A7 Notices to the buyer

The seller must, at the buyer's risk and expense, give the buyer sufficient notice either that the goods have been delivered in accordance with A4 or that the vessel has failed to take the goods within the time agreed.

A8 Delivery document

The seller must provide the buyer, at the seller's expense, with the usual proof that the goods have been delivered in accordance with A4.

Unless such proof is a transport document, the seller must provide assistance to the buyer, at the buyer's request, risk and expense, in obtaining a transport document.

B6 Allocation of costs

The buyer must pay

a. all costs relating to the goods from the time they have been delivered as envisaged in **A4**, except, where applicable, the costs of customs formalities necessary for export, as well as all duties, taxes and other charges payable upon export as referred to in **A6 b**;

b. any additional costs incurred, either because:
   i. the buyer has failed to give appropriate notice in accordance with **B7**, or
   ii. the vessel nominated by the buyer fails to arrive on time, is unable to take the goods, or closes for cargo earlier than the time notified in accordance with **B7**,

   provided that the goods have been clearly identified as the contract goods; and

c. where applicable, all duties, taxes and other charges, as well as the costs of carrying out customs formalities payable upon import of the goods and the costs for their transport through any country.

B7 Notices to the seller

The buyer must give the seller sufficient notice of the vessel name, loading point and, where necessary, the selected delivery time within the agreed period.

B8 Proof of delivery

The buyer must accept the proof of delivery provided as envisaged in **A8**.

A9 Checking – packaging – marking

The seller must pay the costs of those checking operations (such as checking quality, measuring, weighing, counting) that are necessary for the purpose of delivering the goods in accordance with **A4**, as well as the costs of any pre-shipment inspection mandated by the authority of the country of export.

The seller must, at its own expense, package the goods, unless it is usual for the particular trade to transport the type of goods sold unpackaged. The seller may package the goods in the manner appropriate for their transport, unless the buyer has notified the seller of specific packaging requirements before the contract of sale is concluded. Packaging is to be marked appropriately.

A10 Assistance with information and related costs

The seller must, where applicable, in a timely manner, provide to or render assistance in obtaining for the buyer, at the buyer's request, risk and expense, any documents and information, including security-related information, that the buyer needs for the import of the goods and/or for their transport to the final destination.

The seller must reimburse the buyer for all costs and charges incurred by the buyer in providing or rendering assistance in obtaining documents and information as envisaged in **B10**.

B9 Inspection of goods

The buyer must pay the costs of any mandatory pre-shipment inspection, except when such inspection is mandated by the authorities of the country of export.

B10 Assistance with information and related costs

The buyer must, in a timely manner, advise the seller of any security information requirements so that the seller may comply with **A10**.

The buyer must reimburse the seller for all costs and charges incurred by the seller in providing or rendering assistance in obtaining documents and information as envisaged in **A10**.

The buyer must, where applicable, in a timely manner, provide to or render assistance in obtaining for the seller, at the seller's request, risk and expense, any documents and information, including security-related information, that the seller needs for the transport and export of the goods and for their transport through any country.

CFR
COST AND FREIGHT

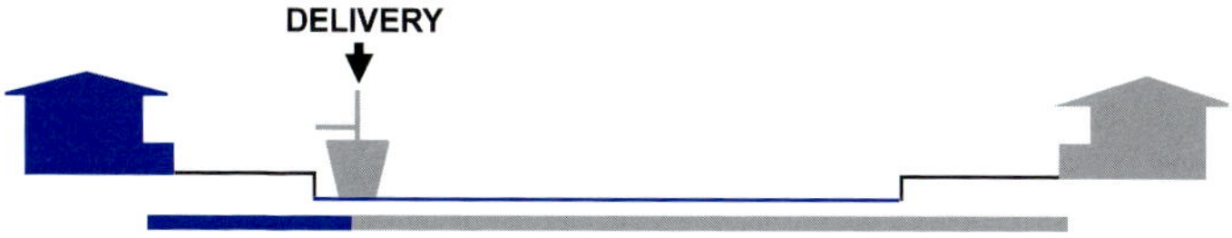

CFR *(insert named port of destination)* Incoterms® 2010

GUIDANCE NOTE

This rule is to be used only for sea or inland waterway transport.

"Cost and Freight" means that the seller delivers the goods on board the vessel or procures the goods already so delivered. The risk of loss of or damage to the goods passes when the goods are on board the vessel. The seller must contract for and pay the costs and freight necessary to bring the goods to the named port of destination.

When CPT, CIP, CFR or CIF are used, the seller fulfils its obligation to deliver when it hands the goods over to the carrier in the manner specified in the chosen rule and not when the goods reach the place of destination.

This rule has two critical points, because risk passes and costs are transferred at different places. While the contract will always specify a destination port, it might not specify the port of shipment, which is where risk passes to the buyer. If the shipment port is of particular interest to the buyer, the parties are well advised to identify it as precisely as possible in the contract.

The parties are well advised to identify as precisely as possible the point at the agreed port of destination, as the costs to that point are for the account of the seller. The seller is advised to procure contracts of carriage that match this choice precisely. If the seller incurs costs under its contract of carriage related to unloading at the specified point at the port of destination, the seller is not entitled to recover such costs from the buyer unless otherwise agreed between the parties.

The seller is required either to deliver the goods on board the vessel or to procure goods already so delivered for shipment to the destination. In addition, the seller is required either to make a contract of carriage or to procure such a contract. The reference to

"procure" here caters for multiple sales down a chain ('string sales'), particularly common in the commodity trades.

CFR may not be appropriate where goods are handed over to the carrier before they are on board the vessel, for example goods in containers, which are typically delivered at a terminal. In such circumstances, the CPT rule should be used.

CFR requires the seller to clear the goods for export, where applicable. However, the seller has no obligation to clear the goods for import, pay any import duty or carry out any import customs formalities.

A THE SELLER'S OBLIGATIONS

A1 General obligations of the seller

The seller must provide the goods and the commercial invoice in conformity with the contract of sale and any other evidence of conformity that may be required by the contract.

Any document referred to in **A1–A10** may be an equivalent electronic record or procedure if agreed between the parties or customary.

A2 Licences, authorizations, security clearances and other formalities

Where applicable, the seller must obtain, at its own risk and expense, any export licence or other official authorization and carry out all customs formalities necessary for the export of the goods.

A3 Contracts of carriage and insurance

a. Contract of carriage

The seller must contract or procure a contract for the carriage of the goods from the agreed point of delivery, if any, at the place of delivery to the named port of destination or, if agreed, any point at that port. The contract of carriage must be made on usual terms at the seller's expense and provide for carriage by the usual route in a vessel of the type normally used for the transport of the type of goods sold.

b. Contract of insurance

The seller has no obligation to the buyer to make a contract of insurance. However, the seller must provide the buyer, at the buyer's request, risk, and expense (if any), with information that the buyer needs for obtaining insurance.

A4 Delivery

The seller must deliver the goods either by placing them on board the vessel or by procuring the goods so delivered. In either case, the seller must deliver the goods on the agreed date or within the agreed period and in the manner customary at the port.

B THE BUYER'S OBLIGATIONS

B1 General obligations of the buyer

The buyer must pay the price of the goods as provided in the contract of sale.

Any document referred to in **B1–B10** may be an equivalent electronic record or procedure if agreed between the parties or customary.

B2 Licences, authorizations, security clearances and other formalities

Where applicable, it is up to the buyer to obtain, at its own risk and expense, any import licence or other official authorization and carry out all customs formalities for the import of the goods and for their transport through any country.

B3 Contracts of carriage and insurance

a. Contract of carriage
The buyer has no obligation to the seller to make a contract of carriage.

b. Contract of insurance
The buyer has no obligation to the seller to make a contract of insurance. However, the buyer must provide the seller, upon request, with the necessary information for obtaining insurance.

B4 Taking delivery

The buyer must take delivery of the goods when they have been delivered as envisaged in **A4** and receive them from the carrier at the named port of destination.

A5 Transfer of risks

The seller bears all risks of loss of or damage to the goods until they have been delivered in accordance with **A4**, with the exception of loss or damage in the circumstances described in **B5**.

A6 Allocation of costs

The seller must pay

a. all costs relating to the goods until they have been delivered in accordance with **A4**, other than those payable by the buyer as envisaged in **B6**;

b. the freight and all other costs resulting from **A3 a**, including the costs of loading the goods on board and any charges for unloading at the agreed port of discharge that were for the seller's account under the contract of carriage; and

c. where applicable, the costs of customs formalities necessary for export as well as all duties, taxes and other charges payable upon export, and the costs for their transport through any country that were for the seller's account under the contract of carriage.

A7 Notices to the buyer

The seller must give the buyer any notice needed in order to allow the buyer to take measures that are normally necessary to enable the buyer to take the goods.

B5 Transfer of risks

The buyer bears all risks of loss of or damage to the goods from the time they have been delivered as envisaged in A4.

If the buyer fails to give notice in accordance with B7, then it bears all risks of loss of or damage to the goods from the agreed date or the expiry date of the agreed period for shipment, provided that the goods have been clearly identified as the contract goods.

B6 Allocation of costs

The buyer must, subject to the provisions of A3 a, pay

a. all costs relating to the goods from the time they have been delivered as envisaged in A4, except, where applicable, the costs of customs formalities necessary for export as well as all duties, taxes, and other charges payable upon export as referred to in A6 c;

b. all costs and charges relating to the goods while in transit until their arrival at the port of destination, unless such costs and charges were for the seller's account under the contract of carriage;

c. unloading costs including lighterage and wharfage charges, unless such costs and charges were for the seller's account under the contract of carriage;

d. any additional costs incurred if it fails to give notice in accordance with B7, from the agreed date or the expiry date of the agreed period for shipment, provided that the goods have been clearly identified as the contract goods; and

e. where applicable, all duties, taxes and other charges, as well as the costs of carrying out customs formalities payable upon import of the goods and the costs for their transport through any country unless included within the cost of the contract of carriage.

B7 Notices to the seller

The buyer must, whenever it is entitled to determine the time for shipping the goods and/or the point of receiving the goods within the named port of destination, give the seller sufficient notice thereof.

A8 Delivery document

The seller must, at its own expense, provide the buyer without delay with the usual transport document for the agreed port of destination.

This transport document must cover the contract goods, be dated within the period agreed for shipment, enable the buyer to claim the goods from the carrier at the port of destination and, unless otherwise agreed, enable the buyer to sell the goods in transit by the transfer of the document to a subsequent buyer or by notification to the carrier.

When such a transport document is issued in negotiable form and in several originals, a full set of originals must be presented to the buyer.

A9 Checking – packaging – marking

The seller must pay the costs of those checking operations (such as checking quality, measuring, weighing, counting) that are necessary for the purpose of delivering the goods in accordance with **A4**, as well as the costs of any pre-shipment inspection mandated by the authority of the country of export.

The seller must, at its own expense, package the goods, unless it is usual for the particular trade to transport the type of goods sold unpackaged. The seller may package the goods in the manner appropriate for their transport, unless the buyer has notified the seller of specific packaging requirements before the contract of sale is concluded. Packaging is to be marked appropriately.

A10 Assistance with information and related costs

The seller must, where applicable, in a timely manner, provide to or render assistance in obtaining for the buyer, at the buyer's request, risk and expense, any documents and information, including security-related information, that the buyer needs for the import of the goods and/or for their transport to the final destination.

The seller must reimburse the buyer for all costs and charges incurred by the buyer in providing or rendering assistance in obtaining documents and information as envisaged in **B10**.

B8 Proof of delivery

The buyer must accept the transport document provided as envisaged in **A8** if it is in conformity with the contract.

B9 Inspection of goods

The buyer must pay the costs of any mandatory pre-shipment inspection, except when such inspection is mandated by the authorities of the country of export.

B10 Assistance with information and related costs

The buyer must, in a timely manner, advise the seller of any security information requirements so that the seller may comply with **A10**.

The buyer must reimburse the seller for all costs and charges incurred by the seller in providing or rendering assistance in obtaining documents and information as envisaged in **A10**.

The buyer must, where applicable, in a timely manner, provide to or render assistance in obtaining for the seller, at the seller's request, risk and expense, any documents and information, including security-related information, that the seller needs for the transport and export of the goods and for their transport through any country.

CIF

COST INSURANCE AND FREIGHT

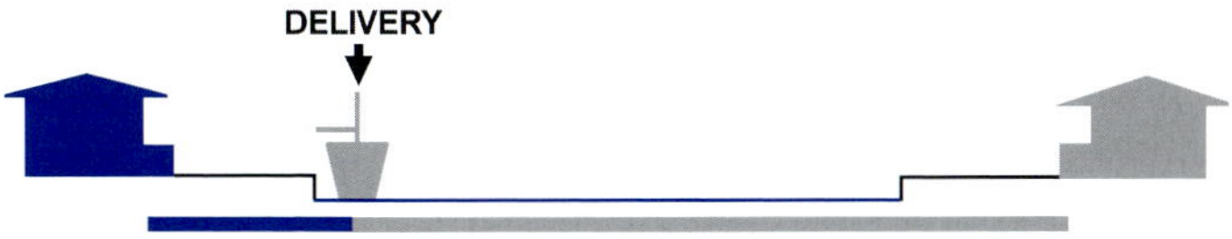

CIF *(insert named port of destination)* Incoterms® 2010

GUIDANCE NOTE

This rule is to be used only for sea or inland waterway transport.

"Cost, Insurance and Freight" means that the seller delivers the goods on board the vessel or procures the goods already so delivered. The risk of loss of or damage to the goods passes when the goods are on board the vessel. The seller must contract for and pay the costs and freight necessary to bring the goods to the named port of destination.

The seller also contracts for insurance cover against the buyer's risk of loss of or damage to the goods during the carriage. The buyer should note that under CIF the seller is required to obtain insurance only on minimum cover. Should the buyer wish to have more insurance protection, it will need either to agree as much expressly with the seller or to make its own extra insurance arrangements.

When CPT, CIP, CFR, or CIF are used, the seller fulfils its obligation to deliver when it hands the goods over to the carrier in the manner specified in the chosen rule and not when the goods reach the place of destination.

This rule has two critical points, because risk passes and costs are transferred at different places. While the contract will always specify a destination port, it might not specify the port of shipment, which is where risk passes to the buyer. If the shipment port is of particular interest to the buyer, the parties are well advised to identify it as precisely as possible in the contract.

The parties are well advised to identify as precisely as possible the point at the agreed port of destination, as the costs to that point are for the account of the seller. The seller is advised to procure contracts of carriage that match this choice precisely. If the seller incurs costs under its contract of carriage related to unloading at the

specified point at the port of destination, the seller is not entitled to recover such costs from the buyer unless otherwise agreed between the parties.

The seller is required either to deliver the goods on board the vessel or to procure goods already so delivered for shipment to the destination. In addition the seller is required either to make a contract of carriage or to procure such a contract. The reference to "procure" here caters for multiple sales down a chain ('string sales'), particularly common in the commodity trades.

CIF may not be appropriate where goods are handed over to the carrier before they are on board the vessel, for example goods in containers, which are typically delivered at a terminal. In such circumstances, the CIP rule should be used.

CIF requires the seller to clear the goods for export, where applicable. However, the seller has no obligation to clear the goods for import, pay any import duty or carry out any import customs formalities.

A THE SELLER'S OBLIGATIONS

A1 General obligations of the seller

The seller must provide the goods and the commercial invoice in conformity with the contract of sale and any other evidence of conformity that may be required by the contract.

Any document referred to in **A1–A10** may be an equivalent electronic record or procedure if agreed between the parties or customary.

A2 Licences, authorizations, security clearances and other formalities

Where applicable, the seller must obtain, at its own risk and expense, any export licence or other official authorization and carry out all customs formalities necessary for the export of the goods.

A3 Contracts of carriage and insurance

a. Contract of carriage

The seller must contract or procure a contract for the carriage of the goods from the agreed point of delivery, if any, at the place of delivery to the named port of destination or, if agreed, any point at that port. The contract of carriage must be made on usual terms at the seller's expense and provide for carriage by the usual route in a vessel of the type normally used for the transport of the type of goods sold.

b. Contract of insurance

The seller must obtain, at its own expense, cargo insurance complying at least with the minimum cover provided by Clauses (C) of the Institute Cargo Clauses (LMA/IUA) or any similar clauses. The insurance shall be contracted with underwriters or an insurance company of good repute and entitle the buyer, or any other person having an insurable interest in the goods, to claim directly from the insurer.

When required by the buyer, the seller shall, subject to the buyer providing any necessary information requested by the seller, provide at the buyer's expense any additional cover, if procurable, such as cover as provided by Clauses (A) or (B) of the Institute Cargo Clauses (LMA/IUA) or any similar clauses and/or cover complying with the

B THE BUYER'S OBLIGATIONS

B1 General obligations of the buyer

The buyer must pay the price of the goods as provided in the contract of sale.

Any document referred to in **B1–B10** may be an equivalent electronic record or procedure if agreed between the parties or customary.

B2 Licences, authorizations, security clearances and other formalities

Where applicable, it is up to the buyer to obtain, at its own risk and expense, any import licence or other official authorization and carry out all customs formalities for the import of the goods and for their transport through any country.

B3 Contracts of carriage and insurance

a. Contract of carriage

The buyer has no obligation to the seller to make a contract of carriage.

b. Contract of insurance

The buyer has no obligation to the seller to make a contract of insurance. However, the buyer must provide the seller, upon request, with any information necessary for the seller to procure any additional insurance requested by the buyer as envisaged in **A3 b**.

Institute War Clauses and/or Institute Strikes Clauses (LMA/IUA) or any similar clauses.

The insurance shall cover, at a minimum, the price provided in the contract plus 10% (i.e., 110%) and shall be in the currency of the contract.

The insurance shall cover the goods from the point of delivery set out in **A4** and **A5** to at least the named port of destination.

The seller must provide the buyer with the insurance policy or other evidence of insurance cover.

Moreover, the seller must provide the buyer, at the buyer's request, risk, and expense (if any), with information that the buyer needs to procure any additional insurance.

A4 Delivery

The seller must deliver the goods either by placing them on board the vessel or by procuring the goods so delivered. In either case, the seller must deliver the goods on the agreed date or within the agreed period and in the manner customary at the port.

A5 Transfer of risks

The seller bears all risks of loss of or damage to the goods until they have been delivered in accordance with **A4**, with the exception of loss or damage in the circumstances described in **B5**.

B4 Taking delivery

The buyer must take delivery of the goods when they have been delivered as envisaged in **A4** and receive them from the carrier at the named port of destination.

B5 Transfer of risks

The buyer bears all risks of loss of or damage to the goods from the time they have been delivered as envisaged in **A4**.

If the buyer fails to give notice in accordance with **B7**, then it bears all risks of loss of or damage to the goods from the agreed date or the expiry date of the agreed period for shipment, provided that the goods have been clearly identified as the contract goods.

A6 Allocation of costs

The seller must pay

a. all costs relating to the goods until they have been delivered in accordance with **A4**, other than those payable by the buyer as envisaged in **B6**;

b. the freight and all other costs resulting from **A3 a**, including the costs of loading the goods on board and any charges for unloading at the agreed port of discharge that were for the seller's account under the contract of carriage;

c. the costs of insurance resulting from **A3 b**; and

d. where applicable, the costs of customs formalities necessary for export, as well as all duties, taxes and other charges payable upon export, and the costs for their transport through any country that were for the seller's account under the contract of carriage.

A7 Notices to the buyer

The seller must give the buyer any notice needed in order to allow the buyer to take measures that are normally necessary to enable the buyer to take the goods.

B6 Allocation of costs

The buyer must, subject to the provisions of **A3 a**, pay

a. all costs relating to the goods from the time they have been delivered as envisaged in **A4**, except, where applicable, the costs of customs formalities necessary for export, as well as all duties, taxes and other charges payable upon export as referred to in **A6 d**;

b. all costs and charges relating to the goods while in transit until their arrival at the port of destination, unless such costs and charges were for the seller's account under the contract of carriage;

c. unloading costs including lighterage and wharfage charges, unless such costs and charges were for the seller's account under the contract of carriage;

d. any additional costs incurred if it fails to give notice in accordance with **B7**, from the agreed date or the expiry date of the agreed period for shipment, provided that the goods have been clearly identified as the contract goods;

e. where applicable, all duties, taxes and other charges, as well as the costs of carrying out customs formalities payable upon import of the goods and the costs for their transport through any country, unless included within the cost of the contract of carriage; and

f. the costs of any additional insurance procured at the buyer's request under **A3 b** and **B3 b**.

B7 Notices to the seller

The buyer must, whenever it is entitled to determine the time for shipping the goods and/or the point of receiving the goods within the named port of destination, give the seller sufficient notice thereof.

A8 Delivery document

The seller must, at its own expense, provide the buyer without delay with the usual transport document for the agreed port of destination.

This transport document must cover the contract goods, be dated within the period agreed for shipment, enable the buyer to claim the goods from the carrier at the port of destination and, unless otherwise agreed, enable the buyer to sell the goods in transit by the transfer of the document to a subsequent buyer or by notification to the carrier.

When such a transport document is issued in negotiable form and in several originals, a full set of originals must be presented to the buyer.

A9 Checking – packaging – marking

The seller must pay the costs of those checking operations (such as checking quality, measuring, weighing, counting) that are necessary for the purpose of delivering the goods in accordance with **A4**, as well as the costs of any pre-shipment inspection mandated by the authority of the country of export.

The seller must, at its own expense, package the goods, unless it is usual for the particular trade to transport the type of goods sold unpackaged. The seller may package the goods in the manner appropriate for their transport, unless the buyer has notified the seller of specific packaging requirements before the contract of sale is concluded. Packaging is to be marked appropriately.

A10 Assistance with information and related costs

The seller must, where applicable, in a timely manner, provide to or render assistance in obtaining for the buyer, at the buyer's request, risk and expense, any documents and information, including security-related information, that the buyer needs for the import of the goods and/or for their transport to the final destination.

The seller must reimburse the buyer for all costs and charges incurred by the buyer in providing or rendering assistance in obtaining documents and information as envisaged in **B10**.

B8 Proof of delivery

The buyer must accept the transport document provided as envisaged in **A8** if it is in conformity with the contract.

B9 Inspection of goods

The buyer must pay the costs of any mandatory pre-shipment inspection, except when such inspection is mandated by the authorities of the country of export.

B10 Assistance with information and related costs

The buyer must, in a timely manner, advise the seller of any security information requirements so that the seller may comply with **A10**.

The buyer must reimburse the seller for all costs and charges incurred by the seller in providing or rendering assistance in obtaining documents and information as envisaged in **A10**.

The buyer must, where applicable, in a timely manner, provide to or render assistance in obtaining for the seller, at the seller's request, risk and expense, any documents and information, including security-related information, that the seller needs for the transport and export of the goods and for their transport through any country.

APPENDIX

ICC AT A GLANCE

ICC is the world business organization, a representative body that speaks with authority on behalf of enterprises from all sectors in every part of the world.

The fundamental mission of ICC is to promote trade and investment across frontiers and help business corporations meet the challenges and opportunities of globalization. Its conviction that trade is a powerful force for peace and prosperity dates from the organization's origins early in the last century. The small group of far-sighted business leaders who founded ICC called themselves "the merchants of peace".

Because its member companies and associations are themselves engaged in international business, ICC has unrivalled authority in making rules that govern the conduct of business across borders. Although these rules are voluntary, they are observed in countless thousands of transactions every day and have become part of the fabric of international trade.

ICC also provides essential services, foremost among them the ICC International Court of Arbitration, the world's leading arbitral institution. Another service is the World Chambers Federation, ICC's worldwide network of chambers of commerce, fostering interaction and exchange of chamber best practice.

Business leaders and experts drawn from the ICC membership establish the business stance on broad issues of trade and investment policy as well as on vital technical and sectoral subjects. These include financial services, information technologies, telecommunications, marketing ethics, the environment, transportation, competition law and intellectual property.

ICC enjoys a close working relationship with the United Nations and other intergovernmental organizations, including the World Trade Organization, the G20 and the G8.

ICC was founded in 1919. Today it groups thousands of member companies and associations from over 120 countries. National committees work with their members to address the concerns of business in their countries and convey to their governments the business views formulated by ICC.

For more information, please visit **www.iccwbo.org**.

ICC DISPUTE RESOLUTION

Incorporating one or more of the Incoterms® rules into a contract does not in itself constitute an agreement to use ICC dispute resolution services. Contracting parties that wish to resort to one or more of these services in the event of a dispute should reach a specific and clear agreement to that effect. For this purpose, ICC offers suggested and standard clauses that parties may incorporate into their contracts. Failing this, parties should agree on the use of ICC rules in an exchange of correspondence.

ICC offers an array of services to help parties overcome disputes arising from international trade. These services respond to different needs and different situations. Each is governed by a set of rules defining a neutral procedure capable of accommodating cultural, linguistic and legal diversity, as well as the specificities of given sectors and activities.

Arbitration, administered by the ICC International Court of Arbitration, generally leads to a binding decision issued by a tribunal of one or three arbitrators. The decision is widely enforceable because of the legal recognition arbitration enjoys in almost all the world's trading nations.

Amicable dispute resolution embraces various methods of dispute resolution that seek a settlement by consensual means. The neutral third party and the parties to the dispute decide on the settlement technique to be used, which may be mediation, neutral evaluation, a mini-trial or a combination of different techniques.

Dispute boards are ongoing bodies set up for the duration of a contract to resolve disputes as and when they arise during the life of the contract. Different types of dispute boards are available, depending on the powers the parties wish to grant to the members of the board and the force of their determinations.

Expertise consists of engaging a specialist to give an opinion on a matter requiring specialist knowledge and skills, such as technical, financial or legal know-how. The services offered range from the search for a suitable expert to the complete administration of the expert's mission. A specific service called DOCDEX is offered for disputes relating to documentary credits, bank-to-bank reimbursements, collections and guarantees.

For further information, including all rules and clauses, visit our dispute resolution pages at **www.iccwbo.org**.

Incoterms® 2010

by the International Chamber of Commerce (ICC)

Die Regeln der ICC zur Auslegung nationaler und internationaler Handelsklauseln

Gültig ab 1. Januar 2011

Die Incoterms® 2010 sind von der Internationalen Handelskammer (ICC) in englisch verabschiedet worden. Sollte die deutsche Übersetzung zur englischen Fassung im Widerspruch stehen, so hat die englische Version Vorrang.

ICC
International Chamber of Commerce
The world business organization

VORWORT

von Rajat Gupta, Präsident der ICC

Die Globalisierung der Wirtschaft eröffnet Unternehmen in einem bisher nicht gekannten Ausmaß den Zugang zu den weltweiten Märkten. Der internationale Handel nimmt stetig an Volumen und Vielfalt, aber auch an Komplexität zu. Kaufverträge müssen diese Entwicklung entsprechend abbilden, um Missverständnissen und kostenintensiven Streitigkeiten vorzubeugen.

Die Incoterms® Regeln, das offizielle Regelwerk der ICC zur Auslegung nationaler und internationaler Handelsklauseln, erleichtern die Durchführung des weltweiten Handels. Durch den Verweis auf die Incoterms® 2010 werden in einem Kaufvertrag die Pflichten der Parteien eindeutig festgelegt und das Risiko rechtlicher Komplikationen vermindert.

Seit der Schaffung der Incoterms® Regeln durch die ICC im Jahre 1936 wurde dieses weltweit anerkannte Standardwerk regelmäßig überarbeitet, um mit den Entwicklungen im internationalen Handel Schritt zu halten. Die Incoterms® 2010 Regeln berücksichtigen die weitere Ausdehnung von Freihandelszonen, den wachsenden Einsatz elektronischer Kommunikationsmittel bei Geschäftsabwicklungen, das erhöhte Bedürfnis nach Sicherheit im Warenverkehr und Veränderungen bei den Transporttechniken. Die Incoterms® 2010 modernisieren und konsolidieren die „Geliefert"- Regeln, verringern die Anzahl von vorher 13 auf nunmehr 11 Klauseln und bieten eine einfachere und klarere Präsentation aller Klauseln. Incoterms® 2010 ist die erste Fassung der Incoterms® Regeln, in der die Begriffe „Verkäufer" und „Käufer" geschlechtsneutral formuliert sind.*

Die umfassende Sachkenntnis der ICC-Kommission für Internationale Handelspraxis, die sich aus Mitgliedern aus allen Teilen der Welt und allen Branchen zusammensetzt, stellt sicher, dass die Incoterms® 2010 den Ansprüchen der Wirtschaft weltweit gerecht werden.

Die ICC möchte den Mitgliedern der Kommission unter Vorsitz von Fabio Bortolotti (Italien) ihren Dank ausdrücken, genauso wie der Incoterms® 2010 Drafting Group, die sich zusammensetzte

* Zur leichteren Lesbarkeit werden in der deutschen Übersetzung die Begriffe „Verkäufer" und „Käufer" verwendet, womit Verkäuferinnen/Verkäufer und Käuferinnen/Käufer gemeint sind.

aus Charles Debattista (Co-Vorsitzender, Großbritannien), Christoph Martin Radtke (Co-Vorsitzender, Frankreich), Jens Bredow (Deutschland), Johnny Herre (Schweden), David Lowe (Großbritannien), Lauri Railas (Finnland), Frank Reynolds (USA) und Miroslav Subert (Tschechische Republik). Darüber hinaus danken wir Asko Raty (Finnland) für die Piktogramme.

Die Incoterms®[1] Regeln dienen der Auslegung einer Reihe von (mit drei Buchstaben abgekürzten) Klauseln, durch die B2B-Handelspraktiken im Kaufvertrag abgebildet werden. Die Incoterms® Regeln beschreiben im Wesentlichen die Pflichten, Kosten und Gefahren, die mit der Lieferung der Ware vom Verkäufer zum Käufer verbunden sind.

Auslegungshinweise für die Incoterms® 2010 Regeln

1. Beziehen Sie die Incoterms® 2010 Regeln ausdrücklich in Ihren Kaufvertrag ein

Wenn Sie möchten, dass die Incoterms® 2010 Regeln für Ihren Kaufvertrag gelten sollen, müssen Sie dies in Ihrem Vertrag deutlich machen, z. B. mit der Formulierung „[*die gewählte Incoterms® Klausel einschließlich des benannten Ortes, gefolgt von*] Incoterms® 2010".

2. Wählen Sie die geeignete Incoterms® Klausel

Bei der Wahl der richtigen Incoterms® Klausel ist zunächst zu beachten, dass sie für Ware und Beförderungsmittel geeignet sein muss; darüber hinaus muss sie alle weiteren Pflichten, die der Verkäufer oder Käufer übernehmen soll, richtig abbilden, wie z. B. wer für die Organisation des Transports oder den Abschluss einer Versicherung verantwortlich sein soll. Der Anwendungshinweis für jede Incoterms® Klausel beinhaltet hilfreiche Informationen, die insbesondere die Auswahl der geeigneten Klausel erleichtern. Die Parteien sollten unabhängig von der verwendeten Incoterms® Klausel stets beachten, dass die Auslegung ihres Vertrags auch von den Gebräuchen des jeweiligen Hafens oder Ortes abhängen kann.

3. Benennen Sie Ihren Ort oder Hafen so genau wie möglich

Die gewählte Incoterms® Klausel kann nur dann ihren Zweck erfüllen, wenn die Parteien einen Ort oder Hafen so genau wie möglich benennen.

Ein gutes Beispiel für eine genaue Definition wäre:

„FCA 38 Cours Albert 1er, Paris, France Incoterms® 2010".

Bei Verwendung der Incoterms® Klauseln „Ab Werk" (EXW), „Frei Frachtführer" (FCA), „Geliefert Terminal" (DAT), „Geliefert benannter Ort" (DAP), „Geliefert verzollt" (DDP), „Frei Längsseite Schiff" (FAS) und „Frei an Bord" (FOB) ist der benannte Ort jener Ort, an dem die Lieferung stattfindet und die Gefahr vom Verkäufer auf den Käu-

1 „Incoterms" ist eine eingetragene Marke der Internationalen Handelskammer (ICC).

fer übergeht. Bei Verwendung der Incoterms® Klauseln „Frachtfrei" (CPT), „Frachtfrei versichert" (CIP), „Kosten und Fracht" (CFR), und „Kosten, Versicherung und Fracht" (CIF) weicht der benannte Ort vom Lieferort ab. Bei diesen vier Klauseln ist der benannte Ort jener Bestimmungsort, bis zu dem die Fracht bezahlt wird. Es kann hilfreich sein, innerhalb eines Ortes oder Bestimmungsortes eine präzise Stelle zu bestimmen, um Zweifel und Streitigkeiten zu vermeiden.

4. Denken Sie daran, dass die Incoterms® Regeln keinen vollständigen Kaufvertrag beinhalten

Die Incoterms® Regeln legen fest, welche Partei des Kaufvertrags die Verpflichtung hat, einen Beförderungs- oder Versicherungsvertrag abzuschließen, wenn der Verkäufer an den Käufer liefert, und welche Kosten jede Partei zu tragen hat. Die Incoterms® Regeln sagen hingegen nichts über den Kaufpreis oder die Zahlungsabwicklung aus. Sie behandeln auch nicht den Eigentumsübergang der Ware oder die Rechtsfolgen eines Vertragsbruches. Diese Angelegenheiten werden normalerweise durch ausdrückliche Vereinbarungen im Kaufvertrag oder durch das diesem Vertrag zugrunde liegende Recht geregelt. Den Parteien sollte bewusst sein, dass das zwingende nationale Recht bestimmte Aspekte des Kaufvertrags, einschließlich der gewählten Incoterms® Klausel, außer Kraft setzen kann.

Hauptmerkmale der Incoterms® 2010 Klauseln

1. Zwei neue Incoterms® Klauseln – DAT und DAP – haben die Incoterms® 2000 Klauseln DAF, DES, DEQ und DDU ersetzt

Die Anzahl der Incoterms® Klauseln wurde von 13 auf 11 reduziert. Dieses wurde durch die Aufnahme von zwei neuen Klauseln – DAT, „Geliefert Terminal", und DAP, „Geliefert benannter Ort" – erreicht. Beide können unabhängig von der vereinbarten Transportart verwendet werden und ersetzen die Incoterms® 2000 Klauseln DAF, DES, DEQ und DDU.

Bei Verwendung der beiden neuen Klauseln findet die Lieferung am benannten Bestimmungsort statt: bei DAT, indem die Ware dem Käufer vom ankommenden Beförderungsmittel entladen zur Verfügung gestellt wird (entsprechend der früheren DEQ-Klausel); bei DAP, indem die Ware dem Käufer entladebereit zur Verfügung gestellt wird (entsprechend den alten DAF-, DES- und DDU-Klauseln).

Die neuen Regeln machen die Incoterms® 2000 Klauseln DES und DEQ überflüssig. Bei Verwendung von DAT kann sich der benannte Terminal auch in einem Hafen befinden, weshalb DAT nunmehr gleichermaßen in den Fällen verwendet werden kann, in denen zuvor die DEQ-Klausel nach den Incoterms® 2000 verwendet wurde. Gleichermaßen kann das ankommende Beförderungsmittel nach DAP ein Schiff und der benannte Bestimmungsort ein Hafen sein: Folglich kann DAP gleichermaßen in den Fällen verwendet werden, in denen früher DES Incoterms® 2000 verwendet wurde. Nach diesen neuen Regeln, wie schon bei ihren Vorgängern, bedeutet „geliefert", dass der Verkäufer alle Kosten (ausgenommen solcher, die mit einer gegebenenfalls erforderlichen Einfuhrgenehmigung verbunden sind) und alle mit der Beförderung der Ware bis zum benannten Bestimmungsort verbundenen Gefahren trägt.

2. Einteilung der 11 Incoterms® 2010 Klauseln

Die 11 Incoterms® 2010 Klauseln sind in zwei unterschiedliche Kategorien aufgeteilt:

KLAUSELN FÜR ALLE TRANSPORTARTEN

EXW	Ab Werk
FCA	Frei Frachtführer
CPT	Frachtfrei
CIP	Frachtfrei versichert
DAT	Geliefert Terminal
DAP	Geliefert benannter Ort
DDP	Geliefert verzollt

KLAUSELN FÜR DEN SEE- UND BINNENSCHIFFS-TRANSPORT

FAS	Frei Längsseite Schiff
FOB	Frei an Bord
CFR	Kosten und Fracht
CIF	Kosten, Versicherung und Fracht

Die erste Kategorie enthält die sieben Incoterms® 2010 Klauseln, die unabhängig von der gewählten Transportart und unabhängig davon, ob mehr als eine Transportart eingesetzt wird, verwendet werden können. EXW, FCA, CPT, CIP, DAT, DAP und DDP zählen zu dieser Kategorie. Sie können auch dann verwendet werden, wenn kein Seetransport stattfindet. Es ist jedoch wichtig festzuhalten, dass diese Klauseln durchaus verwendet werden können, wenn ein Schiff für einen Transportabschnitt genutzt wird.

In der zweiten Kategorie der Incoterms® 2010 Klauseln sind sowohl der Ort der Lieferung als auch der Ort, bis zu welchem die Ware zum Käufer befördert wird, Häfen, weshalb diese Klauseln als „See- und Binnenschiffsklauseln" bezeichnet werden. FAS, FOB, CFR und CIF gehören in diese Kategorie. In den letzten drei Incoterms® Klauseln wurde die Regelung, wonach die Schiffsreling der Lieferort ist, zugunsten der Bestimmung aufgegeben, dass die Ware geliefert ist, sobald sie sich „an Bord" des Schiffs befindet. Dies spiegelt die moderne Wirklichkeit im Handelsgeschäft genauer wider und vermeidet das veraltete Bild, wonach eine Gefahr über einer gedachten senkrechten Linie hin und her schwebt.

3. Klauseln für den nationalen und internationalen Handel

Die Incoterms® Klauseln wurden traditionell bei *internationalen* Kaufverträgen verwendet, bei denen die Ware nationale Grenzen überschreitet. In verschiedenen Teilen der Welt haben jedoch Freihandelszonen, wie etwa die Europäische Union, die Bedeutung der Grenzformalitäten zwischen verschiedenen Staaten erkennbar verringert. Konsequenterweise weist das Cover der Incoterms® 2010 Regeln ausdrücklich darauf hin, dass diese sowohl in internationalen als auch nationalen Kaufverträgen angewendet werden können. Die Incoterms® 2010 Regeln sind daher so zu verstehen, dass die Verpflichtung zur Erledigung von Aus- und Einfuhrformalitäten nur soweit besteht, als eine solche auch tatsächlich erforderlich ist.

Zwei Entwicklungen haben die ICC davon überzeugt, dass ein Schritt in diese Richtung zeitgemäß ist. Erstens verwenden Kaufleute die Incoterms® Klauseln häufig in ausschließlich inländischen Kaufverträgen. Der zweite Grund ist das verstärkte Interesse in den Vereinigten Staaten, die Incoterms® Klauseln im nationalen Handel zu verwenden und sie den früheren Schifffahrts- und Lieferklauseln des Uniform Commercial Code vorzuziehen.

4. Anwendungshinweise

Vor jeder einzelnen Incoterms® 2010 Klausel finden Sie einen Anwendungshinweis. Die Anwendungshinweise erklären die wesentlichen Inhalte jeder Incoterms® Klausel, beispielsweise wann eine bestimmte Klausel verwendet werden sollte, wann die Gefahr übergeht und wie die Kosten zwischen Verkäufer und Käufer verteilt sind. Die Anwendungshinweise sind kein Bestandteil der eigentlichen Incoterms® 2010 Regeln, vielmehr sind sie dazu gedacht, den Anwender präzise und rasch zu der für ein bestimmtes Geschäft geeigneten Incoterms® Klausel zu leiten.

5. Elektronische Kommunikation

Frühere Versionen der Incoterms® Regeln haben jene Dokumente genau bezeichnet, welche durch elektronische Mitteilungen ersetzt werden konnten. Die Artikel **A1/B1** der Incoterms® 2010 Regeln stellen nun jedoch die elektronische Kommunikation der Kommunikation in Papierform gleich, sofern die Parteien dies vereinbaren oder es handelsüblich ist. Diese Formulierung vereinfacht die Entwicklung von neuen elektronischen Abläufen während der gesamten Geltungsdauer der Incoterms® 2010 Regeln.

6. Versicherungsdeckung

Die Incoterms® 2010 Regeln sind die erste neue Fassung der Incoterms® Regeln seit der Revision der Institute Cargo Clauses und berücksichtigen die Veränderungen in diesen Bestimmungen. Die Incoterms® 2010 Regeln ordnen Informationspflichten im Hinblick auf die Versicherung den Artikeln **A3/B3** zu, die die Beförderungs- und Versicherungsverträge behandeln. Diese Bestimmungen wurden aus den allgemeinen „Sonstige Verpflichtungen" der Artikel **A10/B10** der Incoterms® 2000 Regeln herausgenommen. Der Wortlaut der Artikel **A3/B3** im Hinblick auf die Versicherung ist gleichfalls verändert worden, um die Verpflichtungen der Parteien genauer zu definieren.

7. Sicherheitsrelevante Freigaben und hierfür benötigte Informationen

Es gibt heute eine zunehmende Besorgnis über die Sicherheit im Warentransport. Dies macht den Nachweis erforderlich, dass von der Ware keine Gefahr für Leben oder Sachwerte ausgeht, die über das von Natur aus übliche Maß hinausgeht. Daher haben die Incoterms® 2010 Regeln die Verpflichtungen zwischen Käufer und Verkäufer betreffend Erlangung bzw. Unterstützung bei der Erlangung von sicherheitsrelevanten Freigaben in den Artikeln **A2/B2** und **A10/B10** einiger Incoterms® Regeln neu aufgeteilt, beispielsweise hinsichtlich Informationen über die Überwachungskette.

8. Hafenumschlagsgebühren

Nach den Incoterms® Klauseln CPT, CIP, CFR, CIF, DAT, DAP und DDP hat der Verkäufer die Beförderung der Ware zum vereinbarten Bestimmungsort zu organisieren. Frachtkosten werden zwar vom Verkäufer bezahlt, tatsächlich übernimmt sie jedoch der Käufer, da sie üblicherweise im Endverkaufspreis des Verkäufers enthalten sind. Die Beförderungskosten enthalten in manchen Fällen die Kosten für den Umschlag und die Bewegung der Ware innerhalb von Hafen- oder Containerterminalanlagen. Der Frachtführer oder Terminalbetreiber wird diese Kosten möglicherweise dem Käufer berechnen, der die Ware entgegennimmt. Unter diesen Umständen wird der Käufer daran interessiert sein, eine doppelte Zahlung für ein und dieselbe Leistung zu vermeiden, zunächst an den Verkäufer als Teil des Gesamtkaufpreises und noch einmal separat an den Frachtführer oder den Terminalbetreiber. Die Incoterms® 2010 Regeln suchen dies durch eine klare Verteilung solcher Kosten in Artikel **A6/B6** der betreffenden Incoterms® Klauseln zu vermeiden.

9. Verkaufsketten

Im Gegensatz zum Verkauf von Industriegütern werden Rohstoffe häufig während des Transports in einer Verkaufskette mehrmals weiterveräußert. In solchen Fällen „versendet" ein Verkäufer in der Mitte der Kette nicht die Ware, da diese bereits von dem ersten Verkäufer in der Kette versandt wurde. Der Verkäufer in der Mitte der Kette erfüllt deswegen seine Verpflichtungen gegenüber seinem Käufer nicht durch die Versendung der Ware, sondern durch das „Verschaffen" der bereits versandten Ware. Zur Klarstellung schließen die Incoterms® 2010 Regeln die Verpflichtung zur „Verschaffung versandter Ware" als Alternative zu der Verpflichtung ein, die Ware nach den betreffenden Incoterms® Klauseln tatsächlich zu versenden.

Abänderungen von Incoterms® Klauseln

Manchmal möchten die Parteien eine Incoterms® Klausel abändern. Die Incoterms® 2010 Regeln verbieten eine solche Abänderung nicht, jedoch ergeben sich daraus Gefahren. Um unliebsame Überraschungen zu vermeiden, sollten die Parteien die beabsichtigte Wirkung einer solchen Abänderung sehr genau in ihrem Vertrag deutlich machen. Wenn beispielsweise die Verteilung der Kosten in den Incoterms® 2010 Regeln vertraglich abgeändert wird, sollten die Parteien auch klarstellen, ob sie gleichzeitig beabsichtigen, die Stelle des Übergangs der Gefahr vom Verkäufer auf den Käufer abzuändern.

Bedeutung dieser Einführung

Diese Einleitung bietet allgemeine Informationen darüber, wie die Incoterms® 2010 Regeln zu verwenden und interpretieren sind. Sie bildet jedoch keinen Bestandteil dieses Regelwerks.

Erläuterung der in den Incoterms® 2010 Regeln verwendeten Begriffe

Wie in den Incoterms® 2000 Regeln werden die Verkäufer- und Käuferpflichten spiegelbildlich dargestellt. Rubrik **A** beinhaltet die Verpflichtungen des Verkäufers und Rubrik **B** die Verpflichtungen des Käufers. Diese Verpflichtungen können persönlich vom Verkäufer oder Käufer erfüllt werden oder manchmal, unter Berücksichtigung der Bestimmungen des Vertrags oder des anwendbaren Rechts, durch beauftragte Dritte wie Frachtführer, Spediteure oder andere vom Verkäufer oder Käufer für einen bestimmten Zweck benannte Personen.

Der Text der Incoterms® 2010 Regeln versteht sich als selbsterklärend. Um Anwendern gleichwohl Hilfestellung zu leisten, erläutert der folgende Text, wie ausgewählte Begriffe in den Regeln verwendet werden.

Frachtführer: Im Rahmen der Incoterms® 2010 Regeln ist unter einem Frachtführer jene Partei zu verstehen, mit der der Frachtvertrag geschlossen wurde.

Zollformalitäten: Diese Anforderungen sind zur Einhaltung anwendbarer zollrechtlicher Bestimmungen zu erfüllen und können Verpflichtungen zu schriftlicher Dokumentation, Sicherheitsleistungen, Informationsbereitstellung oder Warenkontrolle enthalten.

Lieferung: Dieser Begriff hat im Handelsrecht und in der Handelspraxis mehrere Bedeutungen. Die Incoterms® 2010 Regeln jedoch bezeichnen damit den Ort, an dem die Gefahr des Verlustes oder der Beschädigung der Ware vom Verkäufer auf den Käufer übergeht.

Transportdokument: Dieser Ausdruck wird nunmehr als Überschrift von Artikel **A8** verwendet. Es handelt sich um ein Dokument, das beweist, dass die Lieferung stattgefunden hat. In vielen der Incoterms® 2010 Regeln handelt es sich bei dem Transportdokument um einen Liefernachweis oder einen entsprechenden elektronischen Nachweis. Bei den Klauseln EXW, FCA, FAS und FOB kann es sich jedoch bei dem Transportdokument lediglich um eine Empfangsbestätigung handeln. Ein Transportdokument kann auch weitere Funktionen haben, wie z. B. Teil der Zahlungsabwicklung sein.

Elektronischer Beleg oder Verfahren: Ein Satz von Informationen, bestehend aus einer oder mehreren elektronischen Nachrichten und, falls zutreffend, funktionsgemäß gleichbedeutend mit dem entsprechenden Dokument in Papierform.

Verpackung: Dieser Begriff wird für verschiedene Zwecke verwendet:

1. die Verpackung der Ware entsprechend den vertraglichen Vereinbarungen
2. die Verpackung der Ware, so dass diese transportfähig ist
3. das Verstauen der verpackten Ware innerhalb eines Containers oder innerhalb eines anderen Transportmittels.

Die Incoterms® 2010 Regeln verstehen unter Verpackung sowohl den Inhalt von Punkt 1 als auch Punkt 2. Die Incoterms® 2010 Regeln behandeln nicht die Verpflichtungen der Parteien zur Verstauung innerhalb eines Containers. Daher sollten die Parteien gegebenenfalls Entsprechendes in den Kaufvertrag aufnehmen.

KLAUSELN FÜR ALLE TRANSPORTARTEN

EXW
AB WERK

EXW *(fügen Sie den benannten Lieferort ein)* Incoterms® 2010

ANWENDUNGSHINWEIS

Diese Klausel kann unabhängig von der gewählten Transportart verwendet werden, auch dann, wenn mehr als eine Transportart zum Einsatz kommt. Sie eignet sich für den nationalen Warenhandel, für den internationalen Handel ist hingegen FCA üblicherweise besser geeignet.

„Ab Werk" bedeutet, dass der Verkäufer liefert, wenn er die Ware dem Käufer beim Verkäufer oder an einem anderen benannten Ort (z. B. Werk, Fabrik, Lager usw.) zur Verfügung stellt. Der Verkäufer muss die Ware weder auf ein abholendes Transportmittel verladen, noch muss er sie zur Ausfuhr freimachen, falls dies erforderlich sein sollte.

Die Parteien sind gut beraten, die Stelle innerhalb des benannten Lieferortes so präzise wie möglich zu bezeichnen, da der Verkäufer die Kosten und Gefahren bis zu dieser Stelle zu tragen hat. Der Käufer trägt alle Kosten und Gefahren, die bei der Übernahme der Ware an der gegebenenfalls vereinbarten Stelle am benannten Lieferort entstehen.

EXW stellt die Mindestverpflichtung für den Verkäufer dar. Die Klausel sollte mit Vorsicht angewendet werden, da:

a. der Verkäufer gegenüber dem Käufer keine Verpflichtung hat, die Ware zu verladen, selbst wenn der Verkäufer in der Praxis dazu besser in der Lage wäre. Falls der Verkäufer die Ware verlädt, tut er dieses auf Gefahr und Kosten des Käufers. In Fällen, in denen der Verkäufer besser in der Lage ist, die Ware zu verladen, ist es meist sinnvoller, die FCA-Klausel zu verwenden, da sie den Verkäufer verpflichtet, auf seine Gefahr und Kosten zu verladen.

b. ein Käufer, der von einem Verkäufer auf EXW-Basis zur Ausfuhr kauft, sich bewusst sein sollte, dass der Verkäufer gegenüber

EXW

dem Käufer nicht verpflichtet ist, die Ware für die Ausfuhr freizumachen. Er ist lediglich verpflichtet, den Käufer so zu unterstützen, dass dieser die Ausfuhr durchführen kann. Käufer sind daher gut beraten, EXW nicht zu verwenden, wenn es ihnen nicht möglich ist, direkt oder indirekt die Ausfuhrabfertigung vorzunehmen.

c. der Käufer gegenüber dem Verkäufer nur eine eingeschränkte Verpflichtung hat, diesem Informationen hinsichtlich der Ausfuhr der Ware zur Verfügung zu stellen, obwohl es sein kann, dass der Verkäufer diese Informationen z. B. aus steuerlichen Gründen oder aufgrund von Meldepflichten benötigt.

A VERPFLICHTUNGEN DES VERKÄUFERS

A1 Allgemeine Verpflichtungen des Verkäufers

Der Verkäufer hat die Ware und die Handelsrechnung in Übereinstimmung mit dem Kaufvertrag bereitzustellen und jeden sonstigen vertraglich vereinbarten Konformitätsnachweis zu erbringen.

Jedes Dokument, auf das in **A1–A10** Bezug genommen wird, kann auch ein entsprechender elektronischer Beleg oder ein entsprechendes elektronisches Verfahren sein, wenn dies zwischen den Parteien vereinbart oder üblich ist.

A2 Lizenzen, Genehmigungen, Sicherheitsfreigaben und andere Formalitäten

Falls zutreffend, hat der Verkäufer den Käufer auf dessen Verlangen, Gefahr und Kosten bei der Beschaffung der Ausfuhrgenehmigung oder anderer behördlicher Genehmigungen, die für die Ausfuhr der Ware erforderlich sind, zu unterstützen.

Falls zutreffend, hat der Verkäufer auf Verlangen, Gefahr und Kosten des Käufers diesem alle ihm vorliegenden Informationen, die für die Sicherheitsfreigabe der Ware erforderlich sind, zur Verfügung zu stellen.

A3 Beförderungs- und Versicherungsverträge

a. Beförderungsvertrag
Der Verkäufer hat gegenüber dem Käufer keine Verpflichtung, einen Beförderungsvertrag abzuschließen.

b. Versicherungsvertrag
Der Verkäufer hat gegenüber dem Käufer keine Verpflichtung, einen Versicherungsvertrag abzuschließen. Jedoch hat der Verkäufer dem Käufer auf dessen Verlangen, Gefahr und (gegebenenfalls entstehende) Kosten jene Informationen zur Verfügung zu stellen, die der Käufer für den Abschluss einer Versicherung benötigt.

B VERPFLICHTUNGEN DES KÄUFERS

B1 Allgemeine Verpflichtungen des Käufers

Der Käufer hat den im Kaufvertrag genannten Preis der Ware zu zahlen.

Jedes Dokument, auf das in **B1–B10** Bezug genommen wird, kann auch ein entsprechender elektronischer Beleg oder ein entsprechendes elektronisches Verfahren sein, wenn dies zwischen den Parteien vereinbart oder üblich ist.

B2 Lizenzen, Genehmigungen, Sicherheitsfreigaben und andere Formalitäten

Falls zutreffend, obliegt es dem Käufer, auf eigene Gefahr und Kosten die Aus- und Einfuhrgenehmigung oder andere behördliche Genehmigungen zu beschaffen sowie alle Zollformalitäten für die Ausfuhr der Ware zu erledigen.

B3 Beförderungs- und Versicherungsverträge

a. Beförderungsvertrag
Der Käufer hat gegenüber dem Verkäufer keine Verpflichtung, einen Beförderungsvertrag abzuschließen.

b. Versicherungsvertrag
Der Käufer hat gegenüber dem Verkäufer keine Verpflichtung, einen Versicherungsvertrag abzuschließen.

A4 Lieferung

Der Verkäufer hat die Ware zu liefern, indem er sie dem Käufer am genannten Lieferort an der gegebenenfalls vereinbarten Stelle zur Verfügung stellt, jedoch ohne Verladung auf das abholende Beförderungsmittel. Wurde am benannten Lieferort keine bestimmte Stelle vereinbart und kommen mehrere Stellen in Betracht, kann der Verkäufer die Stelle auswählen, die für den Zweck am besten geeignet ist. Der Verkäufer hat die Ware zum vereinbarten Zeitpunkt oder innerhalb des vereinbarten Zeitraums zu liefern.

A5 Gefahrenübergang

Der Verkäufer trägt bis zur Lieferung gemäß **A4** alle Gefahren des Verlustes oder der Beschädigung der Ware, mit Ausnahme von Verlust oder Beschädigung unter den in **B5** beschriebenen Umständen.

A6 Kostenverteilung

Der Verkäufer hat alle die Ware betreffenden Kosten zu tragen bis diese gemäß **A4** geliefert worden ist, ausgenommen solcher Kosten, die vom Käufer wie in **B6** vorgesehen zu tragen sind.

B4 Übernahme

Der Käufer muss die Ware übernehmen, wenn **A4** und **A7** entsprochen worden ist.

B5 Gefahrenübergang

Der Käufer trägt alle Gefahren des Verlustes oder der Beschädigung der Ware ab dem Zeitpunkt, an dem sie wie in **A4** vorgesehen geliefert worden ist.

Falls der Käufer es unterlässt, gemäß **B7** zu benachrichtigen, trägt der Käufer alle Gefahren des Verlustes oder der Beschädigung der Ware ab dem vereinbarten Lieferzeitpunkt oder ab Ablauf des vereinbarten Lieferzeitraums, vorausgesetzt, die Ware ist eindeutig als die vertragliche Ware kenntlich gemacht worden.

B6 Kostenverteilung

Der Käufer hat:

a. alle die Ware betreffenden Kosten ab dem Zeitpunkt der Lieferung wie in **A4** vorgesehen zu tragen;

b. alle zusätzlichen Kosten zu tragen, die entweder dadurch entstanden sind, dass die ihm zur Verfügung gestellte Ware nicht übernommen worden oder keine Benachrichtigung gemäß **B7** erfolgt ist, vorausgesetzt, die Ware ist eindeutig als die vertragliche Ware kenntlich gemacht worden;

c. falls zutreffend, alle Zölle, Steuern und andere Abgaben sowie die bei der Ausfuhr fälligen Kosten der Zollformalitäten zu tragen; und

d. alle dem Verkäufer durch die in **A2** vorgesehene Unterstützung entstandenen Kosten und Abgaben zu erstatten.

A7 Benachrichtigungen an den Käufer

Der Verkäufer hat den Käufer über alles Nötige zu benachrichtigen, damit dieser die Ware übernehmen kann.

A8 Transportdokument

Der Verkäufer hat gegenüber dem Käufer keine Verpflichtung.

A9 Prüfung – Verpackung – Kennzeichnung

Der Verkäufer hat die Kosten jener Prüfvorgänge (wie Qualitätsprüfung, Messen, Wiegen und Zählen) zu tragen, die notwendig sind, um die Ware gemäß **A4** zu liefern.

Der Verkäufer hat auf eigene Kosten die Ware zu verpacken, es sei denn, es ist handelsüblich, die jeweilige Art der verkauften Ware unverpackt zu transportieren. Der Verkäufer kann die Ware in der für ihren Transport geeigneten Weise verpacken, es sei denn, der Käufer hat den Verkäufer vor Vertragsschluss über spezifische Verpackungsanforderungen in Kenntnis gesetzt. Die Verpackung ist in geeigneter Weise zu kennzeichnen.

A10 Unterstützung bei Informationen und damit verbundene Kosten

Der Verkäufer hat, falls zutreffend, dem Käufer auf dessen Verlangen, Gefahr und Kosten rechtzeitig alle Dokumente und Informationen, einschließlich sicherheitsrelevanter Informationen, die der Käufer für die Aus- und/oder Einfuhr der Ware und/oder für ihren Transport bis zum endgültigen Bestimmungsort benötigt, zur Verfügung zu stellen oder ihn bei deren Beschaffung zu unterstützen.

B7 Benachrichtigungen an den Verkäufer

Wann immer der Käufer berechtigt ist, innerhalb eines vereinbarten Zeitraums den Zeitpunkt und/oder innerhalb des benannten Ortes die Stelle für die Warenübernahme zu bestimmen, hat er den Verkäufer in angemessener Weise darüber zu benachrichtigen.

B8 Liefernachweis

Der Käufer hat dem Verkäufer einen angemessenen Nachweis der Warenübernahme zu erbringen.

B9 Prüfung der Ware

Der Käufer hat die Kosten für jede vor der Verladung zwingend erforderliche Warenkontrolle (pre-shipment inspection) zu tragen, einschließlich behördlich angeordneter Kontrollen des Ausfuhrlandes.

B10 Unterstützung bei Informationen und damit verbundene Kosten

Der Käufer hat dem Verkäufer rechtzeitig alle sicherheitsrelevanten Informationsanforderungen mitzuteilen, so dass der Verkäufer die Verpflichtungen entsprechend **A10** erfüllen kann.

Der Käufer hat dem Verkäufer alle Kosten und Abgaben zu erstatten, die dem Verkäufer durch das Zurverfügungstellen oder die Unterstützung bei der Beschaffung der Dokumente und Informationen wie in **A10** vorgesehen entstanden sind.

FCA
FREI FRACHTFÜHRER

FCA *(fügen Sie den benannten Lieferort ein)* Incoterms® 2010

ANWENDUNGSHINWEIS

Diese Klausel kann unabhängig von der gewählten Transportart verwendet werden, auch dann, wenn mehr als eine Transportart zum Einsatz kommt.

„Frei Frachtführer" bedeutet, dass der Verkäufer die Ware dem Frachtführer oder einer anderen vom Käufer benannten Person beim Verkäufer oder an einem anderen benannten Ort liefert. Die Parteien sind gut beraten, die Stelle innerhalb des benannten Lieferortes so genau wie möglich zu bezeichnen, da an dieser Stelle die Gefahr auf den Käufer übergeht.

Beabsichtigen die Parteien, die Ware beim Verkäufer zu liefern, sind sie angehalten, dessen Adresse als benannten Lieferort anzugeben. Beabsichtigen die Parteien hingegen, dass die Ware an einem anderen Ort geliefert wird, so müssen sie diesen anderen Lieferort genau angeben.

FCA verpflichtet den Verkäufer, falls zutreffend, die Ware zur Ausfuhr freizumachen. Jedoch hat der Verkäufer keine Verpflichtung, die Ware zur Einfuhr freizumachen, Einfuhrzölle zu zahlen oder Einfuhrzollformalitäten zu erledigen.

A VERPFLICHTUNGEN DES VERKÄUFERS

A1 Allgemeine Verpflichtungen des Verkäufers

Der Verkäufer hat die Ware und die Handelsrechnung in Übereinstimmung mit dem Kaufvertrag bereitzustellen und jeden sonstigen vertraglich vereinbarten Konformitätsnachweis zu erbringen.

Jedes Dokument, auf das in **A1–A10** Bezug genommen wird, kann auch ein entsprechender elektronischer Beleg oder ein entsprechendes elektronisches Verfahren sein, wenn dies zwischen den Parteien vereinbart oder üblich ist.

A2 Lizenzen, Genehmigungen, Sicherheitsfreigaben und andere Formalitäten

Falls zutreffend, hat der Verkäufer auf eigene Gefahr und Kosten die Ausfuhrgenehmigung oder andere behördliche Genehmigungen zu beschaffen sowie alle Zollformalitäten zu erledigen, die für die Ausfuhr der Ware erforderlich sind.

A3 Beförderungs- und Versicherungsverträge

a. Beförderungsvertrag

Der Verkäufer hat gegenüber dem Käufer keine Verpflichtung, einen Beförderungsvertrag abzuschließen. Wenn es der Käufer jedoch verlangt oder es Handelspraxis ist und der Käufer keine gegenteilige Anweisung rechtzeitig erteilt, kann der Verkäufer einen Beförderungsvertrag zu üblichen Bedingungen auf Gefahr und Kosten des Käufers abschließen. In beiden Fällen kann es der Verkäufer ablehnen, den Beförderungsvertrag abzuschließen, wovon er den Käufer umgehend in Kenntnis zu setzen hat.

b. Versicherungsvertrag

Der Verkäufer hat gegenüber dem Käufer keine Verpflichtung, einen Versicherungsvertrag abzuschließen. Jedoch hat der Verkäufer dem Käufer auf dessen Verlangen, Gefahr und (gegebenenfalls entstehende) Kosten jene Informationen zur Verfügung zu stellen, die der Käufer für den Abschluss einer Versicherung benötigt.

A4 Lieferung

Der Verkäufer hat die Ware an den Frachtführer oder eine andere vom Käufer benannte Person an der gegebenenfalls vereinbarten Stelle am benannten Ort zum vereinbarten Zeitpunkt oder innerhalb des vereinbarten Zeitraums zu liefern.

B VERPFLICHTUNGEN DES KÄUFERS

B1 Allgemeine Verpflichtungen des Käufers

Der Käufer hat den im Kaufvertrag genannten Preis der Ware zu zahlen.

Jedes Dokument, auf das in **B1–B10** Bezug genommen wird, kann auch ein entsprechender elektronischer Beleg oder ein entsprechendes elektronisches Verfahren sein, wenn dies zwischen den Parteien vereinbart oder üblich ist.

B2 Lizenzen, Genehmigungen, Sicherheitsfreigaben und andere Formalitäten

Falls zutreffend, obliegt es dem Käufer, auf eigene Gefahr und Kosten die Einfuhrgenehmigung oder andere behördliche Genehmigungen zu beschaffen sowie alle Zollformalitäten für die Einfuhr der Ware und für ihre Durchfuhr durch jedes Land zu erledigen.

B3 Beförderungs- und Versicherungsverträge

a. Beförderungsvertrag
Der Käufer hat auf eigene Kosten den Vertrag über die Beförderung der Ware vom benannten Lieferort abzuschließen, es sei denn, der Beförderungsvertrag ist vom Verkäufer wie in **A3a** vorgesehen abgeschlossen worden.

b. Versicherungsvertrag
Der Käufer hat gegenüber dem Verkäufer keine Verpflichtung, einen Versicherungsvertrag abzuschließen.

B4 Übernahme

Der Käufer muss die Ware übernehmen, wenn sie wie in **A4** vorgesehen geliefert worden ist.

Die Lieferung ist abgeschlossen:

a. falls der benannte Ort beim Verkäufer liegt, wenn die Ware auf das vom Käufer bereitgestellte Beförderungsmittel verladen worden ist.

b. in allen anderen Fällen, wenn die Ware dem Frachtführer oder einer anderen vom Käufer benannten Person auf dem Beförderungsmittel des Verkäufers entladebereit zur Verfügung gestellt wird.

Wenn der Käufer am benannten Lieferort keine bestimmte Stelle gemäß **B7 d** mitgeteilt hat und mehrere Stellen in Betracht kommen, kann der Verkäufer jene Stelle auswählen, die für den Zweck am besten geeignet ist.

Sofern der Käufer den Verkäufer nicht anderweitig benachrichtigt, kann der Verkäufer die Ware zur Beförderung in der Weise übergeben, wie es Menge und/oder Art der Ware verlangen.

A5 Gefahrenübergang

Der Verkäufer trägt bis zur Lieferung gemäß **A4** alle Gefahren des Verlustes oder der Beschädigung der Ware, mit Ausnahme von Verlust oder Beschädigung unter den in **B5** beschriebenen Umständen.

B5 Gefahrenübergang

Der Käufer trägt alle Gefahren des Verlustes oder der Beschädigung der Ware ab dem Zeitpunkt, an dem sie wie in **A4** vorgesehen, geliefert worden ist.

Falls

a. der Käufer es unterlässt gemäß **B7**, über die Benennung eines Frachtführers oder einer anderen in **A4** vorgesehenen Person zu benachrichtigen; oder

b. der Frachtführer oder die vom Käufer wie in **A4** vorgesehen benannte Person es unterlässt, die Ware zu übernehmen,

trägt der Käufer alle Gefahren des Verlustes oder der Beschädigung der Ware:

i. ab dem vereinbarten Zeitpunkt oder, mangels eines vereinbarten Zeitpunkts,
ii. ab dem vom Verkäufer nach **A7** mitgeteilten Zeitpunkt innerhalb des vereinbarten Zeitraums; oder, falls kein solcher Zeitpunkt mitgeteilt wurde,
iii. ab dem Ablaufdatum eines vereinbarten Lieferzeitraums,

vorausgesetzt, die Ware ist eindeutig als die vertragliche Ware kenntlich gemacht worden.

A6 Kostenverteilung

Der Verkäufer hat zu tragen

a. alle die Ware betreffenden Kosten bis diese gemäß **A4** geliefert worden ist, ausgenommen solcher Kosten, die wie in **B6** vorgesehen vom Käufer zu tragen sind; und

b. falls zutreffend, die Kosten der für die Ausfuhr notwendigen Zollformalitäten sowie alle Zölle, Steuern und andere Abgaben, die bei der Ausfuhr fällig werden.

A7 Benachrichtigungen an den Käufer

Der Verkäufer hat den Käufer auf dessen Gefahr und Kosten in angemessener Weise darüber zu benachrichtigen, entweder, dass die Ware gemäß **A4** geliefert worden ist, oder dass der Frachtführer oder eine andere vom Käufer benannte Person die Ware innerhalb der vereinbarten Frist nicht übernommen hat.

B6 Kostenverteilung

Der Käufer hat zu tragen

a. alle die Ware betreffenden Kosten ab dem Zeitpunkt, an dem sie wie in **A4** vorgesehen geliefert worden ist, ausgenommen, falls zutreffend, die Kosten der für die Ausfuhr notwendigen Zollformalitäten sowie alle Zölle, Steuern und andere in **A6 b** genannte Abgaben, die bei der Ausfuhr fällig werden;

b. alle zusätzlichen Kosten, die entweder dadurch entstehen, dass:
   i. der Käufer es unterlässt, einen Frachtführer oder eine andere in **A4** vorgesehene Person zu benennen, oder
   ii. der Frachtführer oder die vom Käufer benannte Person wie in **A4** vorgesehen es unterlässt, die Ware zu übernehmen, oder
   iii. der Käufer es unterlässt, gemäß **B7** angemessen zu benachrichtigen,

   vorausgesetzt, die Ware ist eindeutig als die vertragliche Ware kenntlich gemacht worden; und

c. falls zutreffend, alle Zölle, Steuern und andere Abgaben sowie die Kosten der Zollformalitäten, die bei der Einfuhr der Ware fällig werden, und die Kosten für ihre Durchfuhr durch jedes Land.

B7 Benachrichtigungen an den Verkäufer

Der Käufer hat den Verkäufer zu benachrichtigen:

a. rechtzeitig über den Namen des Frachtführers oder einer anderen in **A4** vorgesehenen Person, um dem Verkäufer die Lieferung der Ware gemäß **A4** zu ermöglichen;

b. wenn erforderlich, über den innerhalb des vereinbarten Lieferzeitraums gewählten Zeitpunkt, an dem der Frachtführer oder die benannte Person die Ware übernehmen wird;

c. über die Transportart, die von der benannten Person eingesetzt wird; und

d. über die Stelle der Warenübernahme innerhalb des benannten Ortes.

A8 Transportdokument

Der Verkäufer hat auf eigene Kosten dem Käufer den üblichen Nachweis zu erbringen, dass die Ware gemäß **A4** geliefert worden ist.

Der Verkäufer hat den Käufer auf dessen Verlangen, Gefahr und Kosten bei der Beschaffung eines Transportdokuments zu unterstützen.

A9 Prüfung – Verpackung – Kennzeichnung

Der Verkäufer hat die Kosten jener Prüfvorgänge (wie Qualitätsprüfung, Messen, Wiegen und Zählen), die notwendig sind, um die Ware gemäß **A4** zu liefern, sowie die Kosten für alle von den Behörden des Ausfuhrlandes angeordneten Warenkontrollen vor der Verladung (pre-shipment inspection) zu tragen.

Der Verkäufer hat auf eigene Kosten die Ware zu verpacken, es sei denn, es ist handelsüblich, die jeweilige Art der verkauften Ware unverpackt zu transportieren. Der Verkäufer kann die Ware in der für ihren Transport geeigneten Weise verpacken, es sei denn, der Käufer hat den Verkäufer vor Vertragsschluss über spezifische Verpackungsanforderungen in Kenntnis gesetzt. Die Verpackung ist in geeigneter Weise zu kennzeichnen.

A10 Unterstützung bei Informationen und damit verbundene Kosten

Der Verkäufer hat, falls zutreffend, dem Käufer auf dessen Verlangen, Gefahr und Kosten rechtzeitig alle Dokumente und Informationen, einschließlich sicherheitsrelevanter Informationen, die der Käufer für die Einfuhr der Ware und/ oder für ihren Transport bis zum endgültigen Bestimmungsort benötigt, zur Verfügung zu stellen oder ihn bei deren Beschaffung zu unterstützen.

Der Verkäufer hat dem Käufer alle Kosten und Abgaben zu erstatten, die dem Käufer durch das Zurverfügungstellen oder die Unterstützung bei der Beschaffung der in **B10** vorgesehenen Dokumente und Informationen entstanden sind.

B8 Liefernachweis

Der Käufer hat den wie in **A8** vorgesehen zur Verfügung gestellten Liefernachweis anzunehmen.

B9 Prüfung der Ware

Der Käufer hat die Kosten für jede vor der Verladung zwingend erforderliche Warenkontrolle (pre-shipment inspection) zu tragen, mit Ausnahme behördlich angeordneter Kontrollen des Ausfuhrlandes.

B10 Unterstützung bei Informationen und damit verbundene Kosten

Der Käufer hat dem Verkäufer rechtzeitig alle sicherheitsrelevanten Informationsanforderungen mitzuteilen, so dass der Verkäufer die Verpflichtungen entsprechend **A10** erfüllen kann.

Der Käufer hat dem Verkäufer alle Kosten und Abgaben zu erstatten, die dem Verkäufer durch das Zurverfügungstellen oder die Unterstützung bei der Beschaffung der Dokumente und Informationen wie in **A10** vorgesehen entstanden sind.

Der Käufer hat, falls zutreffend, dem Verkäufer rechtzeitig auf dessen Verlangen, Gefahr und Kosten alle Dokumente und Informationen, einschließlich sicherheitsrelevanter Informationen, die der Verkäufer für den Transport und die Ausfuhr der Ware sowie für ihre Durchfuhr durch jedes Land benötigt, zur Verfügung zu stellen oder ihn bei deren Beschaffung zu unterstützen.

CPT
FRACHTFREI

CPT *(fügen Sie den benannten Bestimmungsort ein)* Incoterms® 2010

ANWENDUNGSHINWEIS

Diese Klausel kann unabhängig von der gewählten Transportart verwendet werden, auch dann, wenn mehr als eine Transportart zum Einsatz kommt.

„Frachtfrei" bedeutet, dass der Verkäufer die Ware dem Frachtführer oder einer anderen vom Verkäufer benannten Person an einem vereinbarten Ort (falls ein solcher Ort zwischen den Parteien vereinbart ist) liefert, und dass der Verkäufer den Beförderungsvertrag abzuschließen und die für die Beförderung der Ware bis zum benannten Bestimmungsort entstehenden Frachtkosten zu zahlen hat.

Werden die Klauseln CPT, CIP, CFR oder CIF verwendet, erfüllt der Verkäufer seine Lieferpflicht, sobald er die Ware dem Frachtführer übergibt und nicht, wenn die Ware den Bestimmungsort erreicht.

Diese Klausel beinhaltet zwei kritische Punkte, da Gefahren- und Kostenübergang an verschiedenen Orten stattfinden. Die Parteien sind gut beraten, im Vertrag sowohl den Lieferort, an dem die Gefahr auf den Käufer übergeht, als auch den benannten Bestimmungsort, bis zu welchem der Verkäufer den Beförderungsvertrag abzuschließen hat, so genau wie möglich anzugeben. Kommen mehrere Frachtführer für die Beförderung zum vereinbarten Bestimmungsort zum Einsatz und verständigen sich die Parteien hinsichtlich der Lieferung nicht auf eine bestimmte Stelle, so geht die Gefahr immer dann über, wenn die Ware dem ersten Frachtführer übergeben worden ist. Die Auswahl der Stelle, an der die Lieferung erfolgen soll, liegt in diesen Fällen gänzlich im Ermessen des Verkäufers, während der Käufer darauf keinen Einfluss hat. Wünschen die Parteien einen späteren Gefahrenübergang (zum Beispiel in einem See- oder Flughafen), dann müssen sie dies in ihrem Kaufvertrag festlegen.

Die Parteien sind außerdem gut beraten, innerhalb des vereinbarten Bestimmungsortes die Stelle so genau wie möglich anzugeben, da die Kosten bis zu dieser Stelle zu Lasten des Verkäufers gehen. Dem

Verkäufer wird geraten, mit dieser Wahl genau übereinstimmende Beförderungsverträge zu verschaffen. Entstehen dem Verkäufer gemäß seinem Beförderungsvertrag Kosten im Zusammenhang mit der Entladung am benannten Bestimmungsort, dann ist der Verkäufer nicht berechtigt, diese Kosten vom Käufer zurückzufordern, sofern nichts anderes zwischen den Parteien vereinbart worden ist.

CPT verpflichtet den Verkäufer, falls zutreffend, die Ware zur Ausfuhr freizumachen. Jedoch hat der Verkäufer keine Verpflichtung, die Ware zur Einfuhr freizumachen, Einfuhrzölle zu zahlen oder Einfuhrzollformalitäten zu erledigen.

A VERPFLICHTUNGEN DES VERKÄUFERS

A1 Allgemeine Verpflichtungen des Verkäufers

Der Verkäufer hat die Ware und die Handelsrechnung in Übereinstimmung mit dem Kaufvertrag bereitzustellen und jeden sonstigen vertraglich vereinbarten Konformitätsnachweis zu erbringen.

Jedes Dokument, auf das in **A1–A10** Bezug genommen wird, kann auch ein entsprechender elektronischer Beleg oder ein entsprechendes elektronisches Verfahren sein, wenn dies zwischen den Parteien vereinbart oder üblich ist.

A2 Lizenzen, Genehmigungen, Sicherheitsfreigaben und andere Formalitäten

Falls zutreffend, hat der Verkäufer auf eigene Gefahr und Kosten die Ausfuhrgenehmigung oder andere behördliche Genehmigungen zu beschaffen sowie alle Zollformalitäten zu erledigen, die für die Ausfuhr der Ware und für ihre Durchfuhr durch jedes Land vor Lieferung erforderlich sind.

A3 Beförderungs- und Versicherungsverträge

a. Beförderungsvertrag

Der Verkäufer hat für die Ware einen Beförderungsvertrag von der gegebenenfalls vereinbarten Lieferstelle am Lieferort bis zum benannten Bestimmungsort oder einer gegebenenfalls vereinbarten Stelle an diesem Ort abzuschließen oder zu verschaffen. Der Beförderungsvertrag ist zu den üblichen Bedingungen auf Kosten des Verkäufers abzuschließen und hat die Beförderung auf der üblichen Route und in der handelsüblichen Weise zu beinhalten. Ist keine bestimmte Stelle vereinbart und ergibt sie sich auch nicht aus der Handelspraxis, kann der Verkäufer die Stelle am Lieferort und am benannten Bestimmungsort auswählen, die für den Zweck am besten geeignet ist.

b. Versicherungsvertrag

Der Verkäufer hat gegenüber dem Käufer keine Verpflichtung, einen Versicherungsvertrag abzuschließen. Jedoch hat der Verkäufer dem Käufer auf dessen Verlangen, Gefahr und (gegebenenfalls entstehende) Kosten jene Informationen zur Verfügung zu stellen, die der Käufer für den Abschluss einer Versicherung benötigt.

B VERPFLICHTUNGEN DES KÄUFERS

B1 Allgemeine Verpflichtungen des Käufers

Der Käufer hat den im Kaufvertrag genannten Preis der Ware zu zahlen.

Jedes Dokument, auf das in **B1–B10** Bezug genommen wird, kann auch ein entsprechender elektronischer Beleg oder ein entsprechendes elektronisches Verfahren sein, wenn dies zwischen den Parteien vereinbart oder üblich ist.

B2 Lizenzen, Genehmigungen, Sicherheitsfreigaben und andere Formalitäten

Falls zutreffend, obliegt es dem Käufer, auf eigene Gefahr und Kosten die Einfuhrgenehmigung oder andere behördliche Genehmigungen zu beschaffen sowie alle Zollformalitäten für die Einfuhr der Ware und für ihre Durchfuhr durch jedes Land zu erledigen.

B3 Beförderungs- und Versicherungsverträge

a. Beförderungsvertrag
Der Käufer hat gegenüber dem Verkäufer keine Verpflichtung, einen Beförderungsvertrag abzuschließen.

b. Versicherungsvertrag
Der Käufer hat gegenüber dem Verkäufer keine Verpflichtung, einen Versicherungsvertrag abzuschließen. Allerdings hat der Käufer dem Verkäufer auf dessen Verlangen die für den Abschluss einer Versicherung notwendigen Informationen zur Verfügung zu stellen.

A4 Lieferung

Der Verkäufer hat die Ware zu liefern, indem er sie an den gemäß **A3** beauftragten Frachtführer zum vereinbarten Zeitpunkt oder innerhalb des vereinbarten Zeitraums übergibt.

A5 Gefahrenübergang

Der Verkäufer trägt bis zur Lieferung gemäß **A4** alle Gefahren des Verlustes oder der Beschädigung der Ware, mit Ausnahme von Verlust oder Beschädigung unter den in **B5** beschriebenen Umständen.

A6 Kostenverteilung

Der Verkäufer hat zu tragen

a. alle die Ware betreffenden Kosten bis diese gemäß **A4** geliefert worden ist, ausgenommen solcher Kosten, die wie in **B6** vorgesehen vom Käufer zu tragen sind;

b. die Fracht- und alle anderen aus **A3 a** entstehenden Kosten, einschließlich der Kosten für die Verladung der Ware und aller Abgaben für die Entladung am Bestimmungsort, die gemäß Beförderungsvertrag vom Verkäufer zu tragen sind; und

c. falls zutreffend, die Kosten der für die Ausfuhr notwendigen Zollformalitäten sowie alle Zölle, Steuern und andere Abgaben, die bei der Ausfuhr fällig werden, und die Kosten für die Durchfuhr der Ware durch jedes Land, die gemäß Beförderungsvertrag zu Lasten des Verkäufers gehen.

B4 Übernahme

Der Käufer muss die Ware übernehmen, wenn sie wie in **A4** vorgesehen geliefert worden ist, und hat sie vom Frachtführer am benannten Bestimmungsort entgegenzunehmen.

B5 Gefahrenübergang

Der Käufer trägt alle Gefahren des Verlustes oder der Beschädigung der Ware ab dem Zeitpunkt, an dem sie wie in **A4** vorgesehen geliefert worden ist.

Falls der Käufer es unterlässt, gemäß **B7** zu benachrichtigen, hat er alle Gefahren des Verlustes oder der Beschädigung der Ware ab dem vereinbarten Lieferzeitpunkt oder ab Ablauf des vereinbarten Lieferzeitraums zu tragen, vorausgesetzt, die Ware ist eindeutig als die vertragliche Ware kenntlich gemacht worden.

B6 Kostenverteilung

Der Käufer hat, vorbehaltlich der Bestimmungen in **A3 a**, zu tragen

a. alle die Ware betreffenden Kosten ab dem Zeitpunkt, an dem sie wie in **A4** vorgesehen geliefert worden ist, ausgenommen, falls zutreffend, die Kosten der für die Ausfuhr notwendigen Zollformalitäten sowie alle Zölle, Steuern und andere in **A6 c** genannte Abgaben, die bei der Ausfuhr fällig werden;

b. alle die Ware betreffenden Kosten und Abgaben während des Transports bis zu ihrer Ankunft am vereinbarten Bestimmungsort, sofern solche Kosten und Abgaben gemäß Beförderungsvertrag nicht zu Lasten des Verkäufers gehen;

c. die Entladekosten, sofern solche Kosten gemäß Beförderungsvertrag nicht zu Lasten des Verkäufers gehen;

d. alle zusätzlichen Kosten, sollte der Käufer die Benachrichtigung gemäß **B7** unterlassen, ab dem für die Versendung vereinbarten Zeitpunkt oder ab Ablauf des hierfür vereinbarten Zeitraums, vorausgesetzt, die Ware ist eindeutig als die vertragliche Ware kenntlich gemacht worden; und

e. falls zutreffend, alle Zölle, Steuern und andere Abgaben sowie die Kosten der Zollformalitäten, die bei der Einfuhr der Ware fällig werden, sowie die Kosten für ihre Durchfuhr durch jedes Land, sofern sie nicht in den Kosten des Beförderungsvertrags enthalten sind.

A7 Benachrichtigungen an den Käufer

Der Verkäufer hat den Käufer zu benachrichtigen, dass die Ware gemäß **A4** geliefert worden ist.

Der Verkäufer hat den Käufer über alles Nötige zu benachrichtigen, damit dieser die üblicherweise notwendigen Maßnahmen zur Übernahme der Ware treffen kann.

A8 Transportdokument

Falls handelsüblich oder falls der Käufer es verlangt, hat der Verkäufer auf eigene Kosten dem Käufer das oder die übliche(n) Transportdokument(e) für den gemäß **A3** vertraglich vereinbarten Transport zur Verfügung zu stellen.

Dieses Transportdokument muss die vertragliche Ware erfassen und innerhalb der zur Versendung vereinbarten Frist datiert sein. Falls vereinbart oder handelsüblich, muss das Dokument den Käufer auch in die Lage versetzen, die Herausgabe der Ware bei dem Frachtführer am benannten Bestimmungsort einfordern zu können, und es dem Käufer ermöglichen, die Ware während des Transports durch Übergabe des Dokuments an einen nachfolgenden Käufer oder durch Benachrichtigung an den Frachtführer zu verkaufen.

Wird ein solches Transportdokument als begebbares Dokument und in mehreren Originalen ausgestellt, muss ein vollständiger Satz von Originalen dem Käufer übergeben werden.

A9 Prüfung – Verpackung – Kennzeichnung

Der Verkäufer hat die Kosten jener Prüfvorgänge (wie Qualitätsprüfung, Messen, Wiegen und Zählen), die notwendig sind, um die Ware gemäß **A4** zu liefern, sowie die Kosten für alle von den Behörden des Ausfuhrlandes angeordneten Warenkontrollen vor der Verladung (pre-shipment inspection) zu tragen.

Der Verkäufer hat auf eigene Kosten die Ware zu verpacken, es sei denn, es ist handelsüblich, die jeweilige Art der verkauften Ware unverpackt zu transportieren. Der Verkäufer kann die Ware in der für ihren Transport geeigneten Weise verpacken, es sei denn, der Käufer hat den Verkäufer vor Vertragsschluss über spezifische Verpackungsanforderungen in Kenntnis gesetzt. Die Verpackung ist in geeigneter Weise zu kennzeichnen.

B7 Benachrichtigungen an den Verkäufer

Wann immer der Käufer berechtigt ist, den Zeitpunkt für die Versendung der Ware und/oder den benannten Bestimmungsort oder die Stelle für die Entgegennahme der Ware innerhalb dieses Ortes zu bestimmen, hat er den Verkäufer in angemessener Weise darüber zu benachrichtigen.

B8 Liefernachweis

Der Käufer hat das wie in **A8** vorgesehen zur Verfügung gestellte Transportdokument anzunehmen, wenn dieses mit dem Vertrag übereinstimmt.

B9 Prüfung der Ware

Der Käufer hat die Kosten für jede vor der Verladung zwingend erforderliche Warenkontrolle (pre-shipment inspection) zu tragen, mit Ausnahme behördlich angeordneter Kontrollen des Ausfuhrlandes.

A10 Unterstützung bei Informationen und damit verbundene Kosten

Der Verkäufer hat, falls zutreffend, dem Käufer auf dessen Verlangen, Gefahr und Kosten rechtzeitig alle Dokumente und Informationen, einschließlich sicherheitsrelevanter Informationen, die der Käufer für die Einfuhr der Ware und/oder für ihren Transport bis zum endgültigen Bestimmungsort benötigt, zur Verfügung zu stellen oder ihn bei deren Beschaffung zu unterstützen.

Der Verkäufer hat dem Käufer alle Kosten und Abgaben zu erstatten, die dem Käufer durch das Zurverfügungstellen oder die Unterstützung bei der Beschaffung der in **B10** vorgesehenen Dokumente und Informationen entstanden sind.

B10 Unterstützung bei Informationen und damit verbundene Kosten

Der Käufer hat dem Verkäufer rechtzeitig alle sicherheitsrelevanten Informationsanforderungen mitzuteilen, so dass der Verkäufer die Verpflichtungen entsprechend **A10** erfüllen kann.

Der Käufer hat dem Verkäufer alle Kosten und Abgaben zu erstatten, die dem Verkäufer durch das Zurverfügungstellen oder die Unterstützung bei der Beschaffung der Dokumente und Informationen wie in **A10** vorgesehen entstanden sind.

Der Käufer hat, falls zutreffend, dem Verkäufer rechtzeitig auf dessen Verlangen, Gefahr und Kosten alle Dokumente und Informationen, einschließlich sicherheitsrelevanter Informationen, die der Verkäufer für den Transport und die Ausfuhr der Ware sowie für ihre Durchfuhr durch jedes Land benötigt, zur Verfügung zu stellen oder ihn bei deren Beschaffung zu unterstützen.

CIP

FRACHTFREI VERSICHERT

CIP *(fügen Sie den benannten Bestimmungsort ein)* Incoterms® 2010

ANWENDUNGSHINWEIS

Diese Klausel kann unabhängig von der gewählten Transportart verwendet werden, auch dann, wenn mehr als eine Transportart zum Einsatz kommt.

„Frachtfrei versichert" bedeutet, dass der Verkäufer die Ware dem Frachtführer oder einer anderen vom Verkäufer benannten Person an einem vereinbarten Ort (falls ein solcher Ort zwischen den Parteien vereinbart ist) liefert, und dass der Verkäufer den Beförderungsvertrag abzuschließen und die für die Beförderung der Ware bis zum benannten Bestimmungsort entstehenden Frachtkosten zu zahlen hat.

Der Verkäufer schließt auch einen Versicherungsvertrag gegen die vom Käufer getragene Gefahr des Verlustes oder der Beschädigung der Ware während des Transports ab. Der Käufer sollte beachten, dass der Verkäufer bei Verwendung von CIP lediglich verpflichtet ist, eine Versicherung mit einer Mindestdeckung abzuschließen. Wünscht der Käufer einen höheren Versicherungsschutz, wird er dies entweder ausdrücklich mit dem Verkäufer vereinbaren oder eigene zusätzliche Versicherungsvorkehrungen treffen müssen.

Werden die Klauseln CPT, CIP, CFR oder CIF verwendet, erfüllt der Verkäufer seine Lieferpflicht, sobald er die Ware dem Frachtführer übergibt und nicht, wenn die Ware am Bestimmungsort ankommt.

Diese Klausel beinhaltet zwei kritische Punkte, da Gefahren- und Kostenübergang an verschiedenen Orten stattfinden. Die Parteien sind gut beraten, im Vertrag sowohl den Lieferort, an dem die Gefahr auf den Käufer übergeht, als auch den benannten Bestimmungsort, bis zu welchem der Verkäufer den Beförderungsvertrag abzuschließen hat, so genau wie möglich anzugeben. Kommen mehrere Frachtführer für die Beförderung zum vereinbarten Bestimmungsort zum Einsatz und verständigen sich die Parteien hinsichtlich der Lieferung nicht auf eine bestimmte Stelle, geht die Ge-

fahr immer dann über, wenn die Ware an den ersten Frachtführer übergeben worden ist. Die Auswahl der Stelle, an dem die Lieferung erfolgen soll, liegt in diesen Fällen gänzlich im Ermessen des Verkäufers, während der Käufer darauf keinen Einfluss hat. Wünschen die Parteien einen späteren Gefahrenübergang (zum Beispiel in einem See- oder Flughafen), dann müssen sie dies in ihrem Kaufvertrag festlegen.

Die Parteien sind außerdem gut beraten, innerhalb des vereinbarten Bestimmungsortes die Stelle so genau wie möglich anzugeben, da die Kosten bis zu dieser Stelle zu Lasten des Verkäufers gehen. Dem Verkäufer wird geraten, mit dieser Wahl genau übereinstimmende Beförderungsverträge zu verschaffen. Entstehen dem Verkäufer gemäß seinem Beförderungsvertrag Kosten im Zusammenhang mit der Entladung am benannten Bestimmungsort, dann ist der Verkäufer nicht berechtigt, diese Kosten vom Käufer zurückzufordern, sofern nichts anderes zwischen den Parteien vereinbart ist.

CIP verpflichtet den Verkäufer, falls zutreffend, die Ware zur Ausfuhr freizumachen. Jedoch hat der Verkäufer keine Verpflichtung, die Ware zur Einfuhr freizumachen, Einfuhrzölle zu zahlen oder Einfuhrzollformalitäten zu erledigen.

A VERPFLICHTUNGEN DES VERKÄUFERS

A1 Allgemeine Verpflichtungen des Verkäufers

Der Verkäufer hat die Ware und die Handelsrechnung in Übereinstimmung mit dem Kaufvertrag bereitzustellen und jeden sonstigen vertraglich vereinbarten Konformitätsnachweis zu erbringen.

Jedes Dokument, auf das in **A1–A10** Bezug genommen wird, kann auch ein entsprechender elektronischer Beleg oder ein entsprechendes elektronisches Verfahren sein, wenn dies zwischen den Parteien vereinbart oder üblich ist.

A2 Lizenzen, Genehmigungen, Sicherheitsfreigaben und andere Formalitäten

Falls zutreffend, hat der Verkäufer auf eigene Gefahr und Kosten die Ausfuhrgenehmigung oder andere behördliche Genehmigungen zu beschaffen sowie alle Zollformalitäten zu erledigen, die für die Ausfuhr der Ware und für ihre Durchfuhr durch jedes Land vor Lieferung erforderlich sind.

A3 Beförderungs- und Versicherungsverträge

a. Beförderungsvertrag
Der Verkäufer hat für die Ware einen Beförderungsvertrag von der gegebenenfalls vereinbarten Lieferstelle am Lieferort bis zum benannten Bestimmungsort oder einer gegebenenfalls vereinbarten Stelle an diesem Ort abzuschließen oder zu verschaffen. Der Beförderungsvertrag ist zu den üblichen Bedingungen auf Kosten des Verkäufers abzuschließen und hat die Beförderung auf der üblichen Route und in der handelsüblichen Weise zu beinhalten. Ist keine bestimmte Stelle vereinbart und ergibt sie sich auch nicht aus der Handelspraxis, kann der Verkäufer die Stelle am Lieferort und am benannten Bestimmungsort auswählen, die für den Zweck am besten geeignet ist.

b. Versicherungsvertrag
Der Verkäufer hat auf eigene Kosten eine Transportversicherung abzuschließen, die zumindest der Mindestdeckung gemäß den Klauseln (C) der Institute Cargo Clauses (LMA/IUA) oder ähnlichen Klauseln entspricht. Die Versicherung ist bei Einzelversicherern oder Versicherungsgesellschaften mit einwandfreiem Leumund abzuschließen und muss den Käufer oder jede andere Person mit einem versicherbaren Interesse an der Ware

B VERPFLICHTUNGEN DES KÄUFERS

B1 Allgemeine Verpflichtungen des Käufers

Der Käufer hat den im Kaufvertrag genannten Preis der Ware zu zahlen.

Jedes Dokument, auf das in **B1–B10** Bezug genommen wird, kann auch ein entsprechender elektronischer Beleg oder ein entsprechendes elektronisches Verfahren sein, wenn dies zwischen den Parteien vereinbart oder üblich ist.

B2 Lizenzen, Genehmigungen, Sicherheitsfreigaben und andere Formalitäten

Falls zutreffend, obliegt es dem Käufer, auf eigene Gefahr und Kosten die Einfuhrgenehmigung oder andere behördliche Genehmigungen zu beschaffen sowie alle Zollformalitäten für die Einfuhr der Ware und für ihre Durchfuhr durch jedes Land zu erledigen.

B3 Beförderungs- und Versicherungsverträge

a. Beförderungsvertrag
Der Käufer hat gegenüber dem Verkäufer keine Verpflichtung, einen Beförderungsvertrag abzuschließen.

b. Versicherungsvertrag
Der Käufer hat gegenüber dem Verkäufer keine Verpflichtung, einen Versicherungsvertrag abzuschließen. Allerdings hat der Käufer dem Verkäufer auf dessen Verlangen die für den Abschluss einer vom Käufer verlangten in **A3 b** vorgesehenen zusätzlichen Versicherung notwendigen Informationen zur Verfügung zu stellen.

berechtigen, Ansprüche direkt bei dem Versicherer geltend zu machen.

Der Verkäufer muss auf Verlangen und Kosten des Käufers, vorbehaltlich der durch den Käufer zur Verfügung gestellten vom Verkäufer benötigten Informationen, zusätzliche Deckung, falls erhältlich, beschaffen, wie z.B. entsprechend den Klauseln (A) oder (B) der Institute Cargo Clauses (LMA/IUA) oder ähnlicher Klauseln, und/oder der Institute War Clauses und/oder der Institute Strikes Clauses (LMA/IUA) oder ähnlicher Klauseln.

Die Versicherung muss zumindest den im Vertrag genannten Preis zuzüglich zehn Prozent (d.h. 110%) decken und in der Währung des Vertrags ausgestellt sein.

Der Versicherungsschutz muss die Ware ab dem Lieferort, wie in **A4** und **A5** festgelegt, bis mindestens zum benannten Bestimmungsort decken.

Der Verkäufer hat dem Käufer die Versicherungspolice oder einen sonstigen Nachweis über den Versicherungsschutz zu übermitteln.

Ferner hat der Verkäufer dem Käufer auf dessen Verlangen, Gefahr und (gegebenenfalls entstehende) Kosten jene Informationen zur Verfügung zu stellen, die der Käufer für den Abschluss einer zusätzlichen Versicherung benötigt.

A4 Lieferung

Der Verkäufer hat die Ware zu liefern, indem er sie an den gemäß **A3** beauftragten Frachtführer zum vereinbarten Zeitpunkt oder innerhalb des vereinbarten Zeitraums übergibt.

A5 Gefahrenübergang

Der Verkäufer trägt bis zur Lieferung gemäß **A4** alle Gefahren des Verlustes oder der Beschädigung der Ware, mit Ausnahme von Verlust oder Beschädigung unter den in **B5** beschriebenen Umständen.

B4 Übernahme

Der Käufer muss die Ware übernehmen, wenn sie wie in **A4** vorgesehen geliefert worden ist, und hat sie vom Frachtführer am benannten Bestimmungsort entgegenzunehmen.

B5 Gefahrenübergang

Der Käufer trägt alle Gefahren des Verlustes oder der Beschädigung der Ware ab dem Zeitpunkt, an dem sie wie in **A4** vorgesehen geliefert worden ist.

Falls der Käufer es unterlässt, gemäß **B7** zu benachrichtigen, hat er alle Gefahren des Verlustes oder der Beschädigung der Ware ab dem vereinbarten Lieferzeitpunkt oder ab Ablauf des vereinbarten Lieferzeitraums zu tragen, vorausgesetzt, die Ware ist eindeutig als die vertragliche Ware kenntlich gemacht worden.

A6 Kostenverteilung

Der Verkäufer hat zu tragen

a. alle die Ware betreffenden Kosten bis diese gemäß **A4** geliefert worden ist, ausgenommen solcher Kosten, die wie in **B6** vorgesehen vom Käufer zu tragen sind;

b. die Fracht- und alle anderen aus **A3a** entstehenden Kosten einschließlich der Kosten für die Verladung der Ware und aller Abgaben für die Entladung am Bestimmungsort, die gemäß Beförderungsvertrag vom Verkäufer zu tragen sind;

c. die aus **A3b** resultierenden Kosten für die Versicherung; und

d. falls zutreffend, die Kosten der für die Ausfuhr notwendigen Zollformalitäten sowie alle Zölle, Steuern und andere Abgaben, die bei der Ausfuhr fällig werden, und die Kosten für die Durchfuhr der Ware durch jedes Land, die gemäß Beförderungsvertrag zu Lasten des Verkäufers gehen.

A7 Benachrichtigungen an den Käufer

Der Verkäufer hat den Käufer zu benachrichtigen, dass die Ware gemäß **A4** geliefert worden ist.

Der Verkäufer hat den Käufer über alles Nötige zu benachrichtigen, damit dieser die üblicherweise notwendigen Maßnahmen zur Übernahme der Ware treffen kann.

B6 Kostenverteilung

Der Käufer hat, vorbehaltlich der Bestimmungen in A3 a, zu tragen

a. alle die Ware betreffenden Kosten ab dem Zeitpunkt, an dem sie wie in A4 vorgesehen geliefert worden ist, ausgenommen, falls zutreffend, die Kosten der für die Ausfuhr notwendigen Zollformalitäten sowie alle Zölle, Steuern und andere in A6 d genannte Abgaben, die bei der Ausfuhr fällig werden;

b. alle die Ware betreffenden Kosten und Abgaben während des Transports bis zu ihrer Ankunft am vereinbarten Bestimmungsort, sofern solche Kosten und Abgaben gemäß Beförderungsvertrag nicht zu Lasten des Verkäufers gehen;

c. die Entladekosten, sofern solche Kosten gemäß Beförderungsvertrag nicht zu Lasten des Verkäufers gehen;

d. alle zusätzlichen Kosten, sollte der Käufer die Benachrichtigung gemäß B7 unterlassen, ab dem für die Versendung vereinbarten Zeitpunkt oder ab Ablauf der hierfür vereinbarten Frist, vorausgesetzt, die Ware ist eindeutig als die vertragliche Ware kenntlich gemacht worden;

e. falls zutreffend, alle Zölle, Steuern und andere Abgaben sowie die Kosten der Zollformalitäten, die bei der Einfuhr der Ware fällig werden, sowie die Kosten für ihre Durchfuhr durch jedes Land, sofern sie nicht in den Kosten laut Beförderungsvertrag enthalten sind; und

f. die Kosten für jede zusätzlich auf Verlangen des Käufers nach A3 und B3 abgeschlossene Versicherung.

B7 Benachrichtigungen an den Verkäufer

Wann immer der Käufer berechtigt ist, den Zeitpunkt für die Versendung der Ware und/oder den benannten Bestimmungsort oder die Stelle für die Entgegennahme der Ware innerhalb dieses Ortes zu bestimmen, hat er den Verkäufer in angemessener Weise darüber zu benachrichtigen.

A8 Transportdokument

Falls handelsüblich oder falls der Käufer es verlangt, hat der Verkäufer auf eigene Kosten dem Käufer das oder die übliche(n) Transportdokument(e) für den gemäß **A3** vertraglich vereinbarten Transport zur Verfügung zu stellen.

Dieses Transportdokument muss die vertragliche Ware erfassen und innerhalb der zur Versendung vereinbarten Frist datiert sein. Falls vereinbart oder handelsüblich, muss das Dokument den Käufer auch in die Lage versetzen, die Herausgabe der Ware bei dem Frachtführer am benannten Bestimmungsort einfordern zu können und es dem Käufer ermöglichen, die Ware während des Transports durch Übergabe des Dokuments an einen nachfolgenden Käufer oder durch Benachrichtigung an den Frachtführer zu verkaufen.

Wird ein solches Transportdokument als begebbares Dokument und in mehreren Originalen ausgestellt, muss ein vollständiger Satz von Originalen dem Käufer übergeben werden.

A9 Prüfung – Verpackung – Kennzeichnung

Der Verkäufer hat die Kosten jener Prüfvorgänge (wie Qualitätsprüfung, Messen, Wiegen und Zählen), die notwendig sind, um die Ware gemäß **A4** zu liefern, sowie die Kosten für alle von den Behörden des Ausfuhrlandes angeordneten Warenkontrollen vor der Verladung (pre-shipment inspection) zu tragen.

Der Verkäufer hat auf eigene Kosten die Ware zu verpacken, es sei denn, es ist handelsüblich, die jeweilige Art der verkauften Ware unverpackt zu transportieren. Der Verkäufer kann die Ware in der für ihren Transport geeigneten Weise verpacken, es sei denn, der Käufer hat den Verkäufer vor Vertragsschluss über spezifische Verpackungsanforderungen in Kenntnis gesetzt. Die Verpackung ist in geeigneter Weise zu kennzeichnen.

B8 Liefernachweis

Der Käufer hat das wie in **A8** vorgesehen zur Verfügung gestellte Transportdokument anzunehmen, wenn dieses mit dem Vertrag übereinstimmt.

B9 Prüfung der Ware

Der Käufer hat die Kosten für jede vor der Verladung zwingend erforderliche Warenkontrolle (pre-shipment inspection) zu tragen, mit Ausnahme behördlich angeordneter Kontrollen des Ausfuhrlandes.

A10 Unterstützung bei Informationen und damit verbundene Kosten

Der Verkäufer hat, falls zutreffend, dem Käufer auf dessen Verlangen, Gefahr und Kosten rechtzeitig alle Dokumente und Informationen, einschließlich sicherheitsrelevanter Informationen, die der Käufer für die Einfuhr der Ware und/ oder für ihren Transport bis zum endgültigen Bestimmungsort benötigt, zur Verfügung zu stellen oder ihn bei deren Beschaffung zu unterstützen.

Der Verkäufer hat dem Käufer alle Kosten und Abgaben zu erstatten, die dem Käufer durch das Zurverfügungstellen oder die Unterstützung bei der Beschaffung der in **B10** vorgesehenen Dokumente und Informationen entstanden sind.

B10 Unterstützung bei Informationen und damit verbundene Kosten

Der Käufer hat dem Verkäufer rechtzeitig alle sicherheitsrelevanten Informationsanforderungen mitzuteilen, so dass der Verkäufer die Verpflichtungen entsprechend **A10** erfüllen kann.

Der Käufer hat dem Verkäufer alle Kosten und Abgaben zu erstatten, die dem Verkäufer durch das Zurverfügungstellen oder die Unterstützung bei der Beschaffung der Dokumente und Informationen wie in **A10** vorgesehen entstanden sind.

Der Käufer hat, falls zutreffend, dem Verkäufer rechtzeitig auf dessen Verlangen, Gefahr und Kosten alle Dokumente und Informationen, einschließlich sicherheitsrelevanter Informationen, die der Verkäufer für den Transport und die Ausfuhr der Ware sowie für ihre Durchfuhr durch jedes Land benötigt, zur Verfügung zu stellen oder ihn bei deren Beschaffung zu unterstützen.

DAT
GELIEFERT TERMINAL

DAT *(fügen Sie den benannten Terminal im Bestimmungshafen/-ort ein)*
Incoterms® 2010

ANWENDUNGSHINWEIS

Diese Klausel kann unabhängig von der gewählten Transportart verwendet werden, auch dann, wenn mehr als eine Transportart zum Einsatz kommt.

„Geliefert Terminal" bedeutet, dass der Verkäufer die Ware liefert, sobald die Ware von dem ankommenden Beförderungsmittel entladen wurde und dem Käufer an einem benannten Terminal im benannten Bestimmungshafen oder -ort zur Verfügung gestellt wird. „Terminal" kann jeder Ort sein, unabhängig davon, ob überdacht oder nicht, wie z.B. ein Kai, eine Lagerhalle, ein Containerdepot oder ein Straßen-, Schienen- oder Luftfrachtterminal. Der Verkäufer trägt alle Gefahren, die im Zusammenhang mit der Beförderung der Ware zum und der Entladung im Terminal im benannten Bestimmungshafen oder -ort entstehen.

Die Parteien sind gut beraten, den Terminal und, wenn möglich, eine bestimmte Stelle innerhalb des Terminals im benannten Bestimmungshafen oder -ort so genau wie möglich zu bezeichnen, da die Gefahr bis zu dieser Stelle der Verkäufer trägt. Dem Verkäufer wird geraten, einen mit dieser Wahl genau übereinstimmenden Beförderungsvertrag zu verschaffen.

Falls die Parteien jedoch des Weiteren beabsichtigen, dass der Verkäufer die mit dem Umschlag und dem Weitertransport der Ware vom Terminal zu einem anderen Ort in Zusammenhang stehenden Gefahren und Kosten tragen soll, dann sollten die Klauseln DAP oder DDP verwendet werden.

DAT verpflichtet den Verkäufer, falls zutreffend, die Ware zur Ausfuhr freizumachen. Jedoch hat der Verkäufer keine Verpflichtung, die Ware zur Einfuhr freizumachen, Einfuhrzölle zu zahlen oder Einfuhrzollformalitäten zu erledigen.

A VERPFLICHTUNGEN DES VERKÄUFERS

A1 Allgemeine Verpflichtungen des Verkäufers

Der Verkäufer hat die Ware und die Handelsrechnung in Übereinstimmung mit dem Kaufvertrag bereitzustellen und jeden sonstigen vertraglich vereinbarten Konformitätsnachweis zu erbringen.

Jedes Dokument, auf das in **A1–A10** Bezug genommen wird, kann auch ein entsprechender elektronischer Beleg oder ein entsprechendes elektronisches Verfahren sein, wenn dies zwischen den Parteien vereinbart oder üblich ist.

A2 Lizenzen, Genehmigungen, Sicherheitsfreigaben und andere Formalitäten

Falls zutreffend, hat der Verkäufer auf eigene Gefahr und Kosten die Ausfuhrgenehmigung und andere behördliche Genehmigungen zu beschaffen sowie alle Zollformalitäten zu erledigen, die für die Ausfuhr der Ware und für ihre Durchfuhr durch jedes Land vor Lieferung erforderlich sind.

A3 Beförderungs- und Versicherungsverträge

a. Beförderungsvertrag
Der Verkäufer hat für die Ware auf eigene Kosten einen Beförderungsvertrag bis zum benannten Terminal im vereinbarten Bestimmungshafen oder -ort abzuschließen. Ist kein bestimmter Terminal vereinbart oder ergibt er sich nicht aus der Handelspraxis, kann der Verkäufer den Terminal im vereinbarten Bestimmungshafen oder -ort wählen, der für den Zweck am besten geeignet ist.

b. Versicherungsvertrag
Der Verkäufer hat gegenüber dem Käufer keine Verpflichtung, einen Versicherungsvertrag abzuschließen. Jedoch hat der Verkäufer dem Käufer auf dessen Verlangen, Gefahr und (gegebenenfalls entstehende) Kosten jene Informationen zur Verfügung zu stellen, die der Käufer für den Abschluss einer Versicherung benötigt.

A4 Lieferung

Der Verkäufer hat die Ware von dem ankommenden Beförderungsmittel zu entladen und sie dann dem Käufer zu liefern, indem er sie an dem gemäß **A3 a** benannten Terminal im Bestimmungshafen oder -ort zum vereinbarten Zeitpunkt oder innerhalb des vereinbarten Zeitraums zur Verfügung stellt.

B VERPFLICHTUNGEN DES KÄUFERS

B1 Allgemeine Verpflichtungen des Käufers

Der Käufer hat den im Kaufvertrag genannten Preis der Ware zu zahlen.

Jedes Dokument, auf das in **B1–B10** Bezug genommen wird, kann auch ein entsprechender elektronischer Beleg oder ein entsprechendes elektronisches Verfahren sein, wenn dies zwischen den Parteien vereinbart oder üblich ist.

B2 Lizenzen, Genehmigungen, Sicherheitsfreigaben und andere Formalitäten

Falls zutreffend, muss der Käufer auf eigene Gefahr und Kosten die Einfuhrgenehmigung oder andere behördliche Genehmigungen beschaffen sowie alle Zollformalitäten für die Einfuhr der Ware erledigen.

B3 Beförderungs- und Versicherungsverträge

a. Beförderungsvertrag
Der Käufer hat gegenüber dem Verkäufer keine Verpflichtung, einen Beförderungsvertrag abzuschließen.

b. Versicherungsvertrag
Der Käufer hat gegenüber dem Verkäufer keine Verpflichtung, einen Versicherungsvertrag abzuschließen. Allerdings hat der Käufer dem Verkäufer auf dessen Verlangen die für den Abschluss einer Versicherung notwendigen Informationen zur Verfügung zu stellen.

B4 Übernahme

Der Käufer muss die Ware übernehmen, wenn sie wie in **A4** vorgesehen geliefert worden ist.

A5 Gefahrenübergang

Der Verkäufer trägt bis zur Lieferung gemäß **A4** alle Gefahren des Verlustes oder der Beschädigung der Ware, mit Ausnahme von Verlust oder Beschädigung unter den in **B5** beschriebenen Umständen.

A6 Kostenverteilung

Der Verkäufer hat zu tragen

a. zusätzlich zu den aus **A3 a** entstehenden Kosten alle die Ware betreffenden Kosten bis diese gemäß **A4** geliefert worden ist, ausgenommen solcher Kosten, die wie in **B6** vorgesehen vom Käufer zu tragen sind; und

b. falls zutreffend, die Kosten der für die Ausfuhr notwendigen Zollformalitäten sowie alle Zölle, Steuern und andere Abgaben, die bei der Ausfuhr fällig werden, und die Kosten für die Durchfuhr der Ware durch jedes Land vor Lieferung gemäß **A4**.

A7 Benachrichtigungen an den Käufer

Der Verkäufer hat den Käufer über alles Nötige zu benachrichtigen, damit dieser die üblicherweise notwendigen Maßnahmen zur Übernahme der Ware treffen kann.

A8 Transportdokument

Der Verkäufer hat auf eigene Kosten dem Käufer ein Dokument zur Verfügung zu stellen, das diesem die Übernahme der Ware wie in **A4/B4** vorgesehen ermöglicht.

B5 Gefahrenübergang

Der Käufer trägt alle Gefahren des Verlustes oder der Beschädigung der Ware ab dem Zeitpunkt, an dem sie wie in **A4** vorgesehen geliefert worden ist.

Falls

a. der Käufer seine Verpflichtungen gemäß **B2** nicht erfüllt, trägt er alle daraus resultierenden Gefahren des Verlustes oder der Beschädigung der Ware; oder

b. der Käufer es unterlässt, gemäß **B7** zu benachrichtigen, trägt er alle Gefahren des Verlustes oder der Beschädigung der Ware ab dem vereinbarten Lieferzeitpunkt oder ab Ablauf des vereinbarten Lieferzeitraums,

vorausgesetzt, die Ware ist eindeutig als die vertragliche Ware kenntlich gemacht worden.

B6 Kostenverteilung

Der Käufer hat zu tragen

a. alle die Ware betreffenden Kosten ab dem Zeitpunkt, an dem sie wie in **A4** vorgesehen geliefert worden ist;

b. alle zusätzlichen Kosten, die dem Verkäufer entstehen, falls der Käufer seine Verpflichtungen gemäß **B2** nicht erfüllt oder es unterlässt, gemäß **B7** zu benachrichtigen, vorausgesetzt, die Ware ist eindeutig als die vertragliche Ware kenntlich gemacht worden; und

c. falls zutreffend, die Kosten der Zollformalitäten sowie alle Zölle, Steuern und andere Abgaben, die bei der Einfuhr der Ware fällig werden.

B7 Benachrichtigungen an den Verkäufer

Wann immer der Käufer berechtigt ist, den Zeitpunkt der innerhalb einer vereinbarten Lieferfrist und/oder die Stelle für die Warenübernahme im benannten Terminal zu bestimmen, hat er den Verkäufer in angemessener Weise darüber zu benachrichtigen.

B8 Liefernachweis

Der Käufer hat das wie in **A8** vorgesehen zur Verfügung gestellte Transportdokument anzunehmen.

A9 Prüfung – Verpackung – Kennzeichnung

Der Verkäufer hat die Kosten jener Prüfvorgänge (wie Qualitätsprüfung, Messen, Wiegen und Zählen), die notwendig sind, um die Ware gemäß **A4** zu liefern, sowie die Kosten für alle von den Behörden des Ausfuhrlandes angeordneten Warenkontrollen vor der Verladung (pre-shipment inspection) zu tragen.

Der Verkäufer hat auf eigene Kosten die Ware zu verpacken, es sei denn, es ist handelsüblich, die jeweilige Art der verkauften Ware unverpackt zu transportieren. Der Verkäufer kann die Ware in der für ihren Transport geeigneten Weise verpacken, es sei denn, der Käufer hat den Verkäufer vor Vertragsschluss über spezifische Verpackungsanforderungen in Kenntnis gesetzt. Die Verpackung ist in geeigneter Weise zu kennzeichnen.

A10 Unterstützung bei Informationen und damit verbundene Kosten

Der Verkäufer hat, falls zutreffend, dem Käufer auf dessen Verlangen, Gefahr und Kosten rechtzeitig alle Dokumente und Informationen, einschließlich sicherheitsrelevanter Informationen, die der Käufer für die Einfuhr der Ware und/oder für ihren Transport bis zum endgültigen Bestimmungsort benötigt, zur Verfügung zu stellen oder ihn bei deren Beschaffung zu unterstützen.

Der Verkäufer hat dem Käufer alle Kosten und Abgaben zu erstatten, die dem Käufer durch das Zurverfügungstellen oder die Unterstützung bei der Beschaffung der in **B10** vorgesehenen Dokumente und Informationen entstanden sind.

B9 Prüfung der Ware

Der Käufer hat die Kosten für jede vor der Verladung zwingend erforderliche Warenkontrolle (pre-shipment inspection) zu tragen, mit Ausnahme behördlich angeordneter Kontrollen des Ausfuhrlandes.

B10 Unterstützung bei Informationen und damit verbundene Kosten

Der Käufer hat dem Verkäufer rechtzeitig alle sicherheitsrelevanten Informationsanforderungen mitzuteilen, so dass der Verkäufer die Verpflichtungen entsprechend **A10** erfüllen kann.

Der Käufer hat dem Verkäufer alle Kosten und Abgaben zu erstatten, die dem Verkäufer durch das Zurverfügungstellen oder die Unterstützung bei der Beschaffung der Dokumente und Informationen wie in **A10** vorgesehen entstanden sind.

Der Käufer hat, falls zutreffend, dem Verkäufer rechtzeitig auf dessen Verlangen, Gefahr und Kosten alle Dokumente und Informationen, einschließlich sicherheitsrelevanter Informationen, die der Verkäufer für den Transport und die Ausfuhr der Ware sowie für ihre Durchfuhr durch jedes Land benötigt, zur Verfügung zu stellen oder ihn bei deren Beschaffung zu unterstützen.

DAP
GELIEFERT BENANNTER ORT

DAP *(fügen Sie den benannten Bestimmungsort ein)* Incoterms® 2010

ANWENDUNGSHINWEIS

Diese Klausel kann unabhängig von der gewählten Transportart verwendet werden, auch dann, wenn mehr als eine Transportart zum Einsatz kommt.

„Geliefert benannter Ort" bedeutet, dass der Verkäufer liefert, wenn die Ware dem Käufer auf dem ankommenden Beförderungsmittel entladebereit am benannten Bestimmungsort zur Verfügung gestellt wird. Der Verkäufer trägt alle Gefahren, die im Zusammenhang mit der Beförderung zum benannten Ort stehen.

Die Parteien sind gut beraten, die Stelle innerhalb des benannten Bestimmungsortes so genau wie möglich zu bezeichnen, da die Gefahren bis zu dieser Stelle zu Lasten des Verkäufers gehen. Dem Verkäufer wird geraten, mit dieser Wahl genau übereinstimmende Beförderungsverträge zu verschaffen. Entstehen dem Verkäufer gemäß seinem Beförderungsvertrag Kosten im Zusammenhang mit der Entladung am Bestimmungsort, dann ist der Verkäufer nicht berechtigt, diese Kosten vom Käufer zurückzufordern, sofern nichts anderes zwischen den Parteien vereinbart ist.

DAP verpflichtet den Verkäufer, falls zutreffend, die Ware zur Ausfuhr freizumachen. Jedoch hat der Verkäufer keine Verpflichtung, die Ware zur Einfuhr freizumachen, Einfuhrzölle zu zahlen oder Einfuhrzollformalitäten zu erledigen. Falls die Parteien wünschen, dass der Verkäufer die Ware zur Einfuhr freimacht, Einfuhrzölle zahlt und die Einfuhrzollformalitäten erledigt, sollte die DDP-Klausel verwendet werden.

A VERPFLICHTUNGEN DES VERKÄUFERS

A1 Allgemeine Verpflichtungen des Verkäufers

Der Verkäufer hat die Ware und die Handelsrechnung in Übereinstimmung mit dem Kaufvertrag bereitzustellen und jeden sonstigen vertraglich vereinbarten Konformitätsnachweis zu erbringen.

Jedes Dokument, auf das in **A1–A10** Bezug genommen wird, kann auch ein entsprechender elektronischer Beleg oder ein entsprechendes elektronisches Verfahren sein, wenn dies zwischen den Parteien vereinbart oder üblich ist.

A2 Lizenzen, Genehmigungen, Sicherheitsfreigaben und andere Formalitäten

Falls zutreffend, hat der Verkäufer auf eigene Gefahr und Kosten die Ausfuhrgenehmigung und andere behördliche Genehmigungen zu beschaffen sowie alle Zollformalitäten zu erledigen, die für die Ausfuhr der Ware und für ihre Durchfuhr durch jedes Land vor Lieferung erforderlich sind.

A3 Beförderungs- und Versicherungsverträge

a. Beförderungsvertrag
Der Verkäufer hat für die Ware auf eigene Kosten einen Beförderungsvertrag bis zum benannten Bestimmungsort oder zu der gegebenenfalls vereinbarten Stelle am benannten Bestimmungsort abzuschließen. Ist keine bestimmte Stelle vereinbart oder ergibt sie sich nicht aus der Handelspraxis, kann der Verkäufer jene Stelle am benannten Bestimmungsort auswählen, die für den Zweck am besten geeignet ist.

b. Versicherungsvertrag
Der Verkäufer hat gegenüber dem Käufer keine Verpflichtung, einen Versicherungsvertrag abzuschließen. Jedoch hat der Verkäufer dem Käufer auf dessen Verlangen, Gefahr und (gegebenenfalls entstehende) Kosten jene Informationen zur Verfügung zu stellen, die der Käufer für den Abschluss einer Versicherung benötigt.

A4 Lieferung

Der Verkäufer hat die Ware zu liefern, indem er sie dem Käufer auf dem ankommenden Beförderungsmittel entladebereit am benannten Bestimmungsort an der gegebenfalls vereinbarten Stelle zum vereinbarten Zeitpunkt oder innerhalb des vereinbarten Zeitraums zur Verfügung stellt.

B VERPFLICHTUNGEN DES KÄUFERS

B1 Allgemeine Verpflichtungen des Käufers

Der Käufer hat den im Kaufvertrag genannten Preis der Ware zu zahlen.

Jedes Dokument, auf das in **B1–B10** Bezug genommen wird, kann auch ein entsprechender elektronischer Beleg oder ein entsprechendes elektronisches Verfahren sein, wenn dies zwischen den Parteien vereinbart oder üblich ist.

B2 Lizenzen, Genehmigungen, Sicherheitsfreigaben und andere Formalitäten

Falls zutreffend, muss der Käufer auf eigene Gefahr und Kosten die Einfuhrgenehmigung oder andere behördliche Genehmigungen beschaffen, sowie alle Zollformalitäten für die Einfuhr der Ware erledigen.

B3 Beförderungs- und Versicherungsverträge

a. Beförderungsvertrag
Der Käufer hat gegenüber dem Verkäufer keine Verpflichtung, einen Beförderungsvertrag abzuschließen.

b. Versicherungsvertrag
Der Käufer hat gegenüber dem Verkäufer keine Verpflichtung, einen Versicherungsvertrag abzuschließen. Allerdings hat der Käufer dem Verkäufer auf dessen Verlangen die für den Abschluss einer Versicherung notwendigen Informationen zur Verfügung zu stellen.

B4 Übernahme

Der Käufer muss die Ware übernehmen, wenn sie wie in **A4** vorgesehen geliefert worden ist.

A5 Gefahrenübergang

Der Verkäufer trägt bis zur Lieferung gemäß **A4** alle Gefahren des Verlustes oder der Beschädigung der Ware, mit Ausnahme von Verlust oder Beschädigung unter den in **B5** beschriebenen Umständen.

A6 Kostenverteilung

Der Verkäufer hat zu tragen

a. zusätzlich zu den aus **A3 a** entstehenden Kosten alle die Ware betreffenden Kosten bis diese gemäß **A4** geliefert worden ist, ausgenommen solcher Kosten, die wie in **B6** vorgesehen vom Käufer zu tragen sind;

b. alle Abgaben für die Entladung am Bestimmungsort, die gemäß Beförderungsvertrag vom Verkäufer zu tragen sind; und

c. falls zutreffend, die Kosten der für die Ausfuhr notwendigen Zollformalitäten sowie alle Zölle, Steuern und andere Abgaben, die bei der Ausfuhr fällig werden, und die Kosten für die Durchfuhr der Ware durch jedes Land vor Lieferung gemäß **A4**.

A7 Benachrichtigungen an den Käufer

Der Verkäufer hat den Käufer über alles Nötige zu benachrichtigen, damit dieser die üblicherweise notwendigen Maßnahmen zur Übernahme der Ware treffen kann.

B5 Gefahrenübergang

Der Käufer trägt alle Gefahren des Verlustes oder der Beschädigung der Ware ab dem Zeitpunkt, an dem sie wie in **A4** vorgesehen geliefert worden ist.

Falls

a. der Käufer seine Verpflichtungen gemäß **B2** nicht erfüllt, trägt er alle daraus resultierenden Gefahren des Verlustes oder der Beschädigung der Ware; oder

b. der Käufer es unterlässt, gemäß **B7** zu benachrichtigen, trägt er alle Gefahren des Verlustes oder der Beschädigung der Ware ab dem vereinbarten Lieferzeitpunkt oder ab Ablauf des vereinbarten Lieferzeitraums,

vorausgesetzt, die Ware ist eindeutig als die vertragliche Ware kenntlich gemacht worden.

B6 Kostenverteilung

Der Käufer hat zu tragen

a. alle die Ware betreffenden Kosten ab dem Zeitpunkt, an dem sie wie in **A4** vorgesehen geliefert worden ist;

b. alle Entladekosten, die erforderlich sind, um die Ware vom ankommenden Beförderungsmittel am benannten Bestimmungsort zu übernehmen, sofern diese Kosten gemäß Beförderungsvertrag nicht zu Lasten des Verkäufers gehen;

c. alle zusätzlichen Kosten, die dem Verkäufer entstehen, falls der Käufer seine Verpflichtungen gemäß **B2** nicht erfüllt oder es unterlässt, gemäß **B7** zu benachrichtigen, vorausgesetzt, die Ware ist eindeutig als die vertragliche Ware kenntlich gemacht worden; und

d. falls zutreffend, die Kosten für die Zollformalitäten sowie alle Zölle, Steuern und andere Abgaben, die bei der Einfuhr der Ware fällig werden.

B7 Benachrichtigungen an den Verkäufer

Wann immer der Käufer berechtigt ist, den Zeitpunkt innerhalb einer vereinbarten Lieferfrist und/oder die Stelle für die Warenübernahme am benannten Bestimmungsort zu bestimmen, hat er den Verkäufer in angemessener Weise darüber zu benachrichtigen.

A8 Transportdokument

Der Verkäufer hat auf eigene Kosten dem Käufer ein Dokument zur Verfügung zu stellen, das diesem die Übernahme der Ware wie in **A4/B4** vorgesehen ermöglicht.

A9 Prüfung – Verpackung – Kennzeichnung

Der Verkäufer hat die Kosten jener Prüfvorgänge (wie Qualitätsprüfung, Messen, Wiegen und Zählen), die notwendig sind, um die Ware gemäß **A4** zu liefern, sowie die Kosten für alle von den Behörden des Ausfuhrlandes angeordneten Warenkontrollen vor der Verladung (pre-shipment inspection) zu tragen.

Der Verkäufer hat auf eigene Kosten die Ware zu verpacken, es sei denn, es ist handelsüblich, die jeweilige Art der verkauften Ware unverpackt zu transportieren. Der Verkäufer kann die Ware in der für ihren Transport geeigneten Weise verpacken, es sei denn, der Käufer hat den Verkäufer vor Vertragsschluss über spezifische Verpackungsanforderungen in Kenntnis gesetzt. Die Verpackung ist in geeigneter Weise zu kennzeichnen.

A10 Unterstützung bei Informationen und damit verbundene Kosten

Der Verkäufer hat, falls zutreffend, dem Käufer auf dessen Verlangen, Gefahr und Kosten rechtzeitig alle Dokumente und Informationen, einschließlich sicherheitsrelevanter Informationen, die der Käufer für die Einfuhr der Ware und/oder für ihren Transport bis zum endgültigen Bestimmungsort benötigt, zur Verfügung zu stellen oder ihn bei deren Beschaffung zu unterstützen.

Der Verkäufer hat dem Käufer alle Kosten und Abgaben zu erstatten, die dem Käufer durch das Zurverfügungstellen oder die Unterstützung bei der Beschaffung der in **B10** vorgesehenen Dokumente und Informationen entstanden sind.

B8 Liefernachweis

Der Käufer hat das wie in **A8** vorgesehen zur Verfügung gestellte Transportdokument anzunehmen.

B9 Prüfung der Ware

Der Käufer hat die Kosten für jede vor der Verladung zwingend erforderliche Warenkontrolle (pre-shipment inspection) zu tragen, mit Ausnahme behördlich angeordneter Kontrollen des Ausfuhrlandes.

B10 Unterstützung bei Informationen und damit verbundene Kosten

Der Käufer hat dem Verkäufer rechtzeitig alle sicherheitsrelevanten Informationsanforderungen mitzuteilen, so dass der Verkäufer die Verpflichtungen entsprechend **A10** erfüllen kann.

Der Käufer hat dem Verkäufer alle Kosten und Abgaben zu erstatten, die dem Verkäufer durch das Zurverfügungstellen oder die Unterstützung bei der Beschaffung der Dokumente und Informationen wie in **A10** vorgesehen entstanden sind.

Der Käufer hat, falls zutreffend, dem Verkäufer rechtzeitig auf dessen Verlangen, Gefahr und Kosten alle Dokumente und Informationen, einschließlich sicherheitsrelevanter Informationen, die der Verkäufer für den Transport und die Ausfuhr der Ware sowie für ihre Durchfuhr durch jedes Land benötigt, zur Verfügung zu stellen oder ihn bei deren Beschaffung zu unterstützen.

DDP
GELIEFERT VERZOLLT

DDP *(fügen Sie den benannten Bestimmungsort ein)* Incoterms® 2010

ANWENDUNGSHINWEIS

Diese Klausel kann unabhängig von der gewählten Transportart verwendet werden, auch dann, wenn mehr als eine Transportart zum Einsatz kommt.

„Geliefert verzollt“ bedeutet, dass der Verkäufer liefert, wenn er die zur Einfuhr freigemachte Ware dem Käufer auf dem ankommenden Beförderungsmittel entladebereit am benannten Bestimmungsort zur Verfügung stellt. Der Verkäufer trägt alle Kosten und Gefahren, die im Zusammenhang mit der Beförderung der Ware bis zum Bestimmungsort stehen und hat die Verpflichtung, die Ware nicht nur für die Ausfuhr, sondern auch für die Einfuhr freizumachen, alle Abgaben sowohl für die Aus- als auch für die Einfuhr zu zahlen sowie alle Zollformalitäten zu erledigen.

DDP stellt die Maximalverpflichtung für den Verkäufer dar.

Die Parteien sind gut beraten, die Stelle innerhalb des benannten Bestimmungsortes so genau wie möglich zu bezeichnen, da die Kosten und Gefahren bis zu dieser Stelle vom Verkäufer zu tragen sind. Dem Verkäufer wird geraten, mit dieser Wahl genau übereinstimmende Beförderungsverträge zu verschaffen. Entstehen dem Verkäufer gemäß seinem Beförderungsvertrag Kosten im Zusammenhang mit der Entladung am Bestimmungsort, dann ist der Verkäufer nicht berechtigt, diese Kosten vom Käufer zurückzufordern, sofern nichts anderes zwischen den Parteien vereinbart ist.

Die Parteien sind gut beraten, DDP nicht zu verwenden, wenn der Verkäufer nicht in der Lage ist, direkt oder indirekt die Einfuhrabfertigung zu erledigen.

Wenn die Parteien wünschen, dass der Käufer alle Gefahren und Kosten der Einfuhrabfertigung trägt, sollte die DAP-Klausel verwendet werden.

Alle Mehrwertsteuern und andere im Zusammenhang mit der Einfuhr anfallende Steuern gehen zu Lasten des Verkäufers, sofern nicht ausdrücklich etwas anderes im Kaufvertrag vereinbart wurde.

A VERPFLICHTUNGEN DES VERKÄUFERS

A1 Allgemeine Verpflichtungen des Verkäufers

Der Verkäufer hat die Ware und die Handelsrechnung in Übereinstimmung mit dem Kaufvertrag bereitzustellen und jeden sonstigen vertraglich vereinbarten Konformitätsnachweis zu erbringen.

Jedes Dokument, auf das in **A1–A10** Bezug genommen wird, kann auch ein entsprechender elektronischer Beleg oder ein entsprechendes elektronisches Verfahren sein, wenn dies zwischen den Parteien vereinbart oder üblich ist.

A2 Lizenzen, Genehmigungen, Sicherheitsfreigaben und andere Formalitäten

Falls zutreffend, hat der Verkäufer auf eigene Gefahr und Kosten die Aus- und Einfuhrgenehmigung und andere behördliche Genehmigungen zu beschaffen sowie alle Zollformalitäten zu erledigen, die für die Ausfuhr der Ware, ihre Durchfuhr durch jedes Land und ihre Einfuhr erforderlich sind.

A3 Beförderungs- und Versicherungsverträge

a. Beförderungsvertrag

Der Verkäufer hat für die Ware auf eigene Kosten einen Beförderungsvertrag bis zum benannten Bestimmungsort oder zu der gegebenenfalls vereinbarten Stelle am benannten Bestimmungsort abzuschließen. Ist keine bestimmte Stelle vereinbart oder ergibt sie sich nicht aus der Handelspraxis, kann der Verkäufer jene Stelle am benannten Bestimmungsort auswählen, die für den Zweck am besten geeignet ist.

b. Versicherungsvertrag

Der Verkäufer hat gegenüber dem Käufer keine Verpflichtung, einen Versicherungsvertrag abzuschließen. Jedoch hat der Verkäufer dem Käufer auf dessen Verlangen, Gefahr und (gegebenenfalls entstehende) Kosten jene Informationen zur Verfügung zu stellen, die der Käufer für den Abschluss einer Versicherung benötigt.

A4 Lieferung

Der Verkäufer hat die Ware zu liefern, indem er sie dem Käufer auf dem ankommenden Beförderungsmittel entladebereit am benannten Bestimmungsort an der gegebenfalls vereinbarten Stelle zum vereinbarten Zeitpunkt oder innerhalb des vereinbarten Zeitraums zur Verfügung stellt.

B VERPFLICHTUNGEN DES KÄUFERS

B1 Allgemeine Verpflichtungen des Käufers

Der Käufer hat den im Kaufvertrag genannten Preis der Ware zu zahlen.

Jedes Dokument, auf das in **B1–B10** Bezug genommen wird, kann auch ein entsprechender elektronischer Beleg oder ein entsprechendes elektronisches Verfahren sein, wenn dies zwischen den Parteien vereinbart oder üblich ist.

B2 Lizenzen, Genehmigungen, Sicherheitsfreigaben und andere Formalitäten

Falls zutreffend, muss der Käufer den Verkäufer auf dessen Verlangen, Gefahr und Kosten dabei unterstützen, die Einfuhrgenehmigung oder andere behördliche Genehmigungen für die Einfuhr der Ware zu beschaffen.

B3 Beförderungs- und Versicherungsverträge

a. Beförderungsvertrag
Der Käufer hat gegenüber dem Verkäufer keine Verpflichtung, einen Beförderungsvertrag abzuschließen.

b. Versicherungsvertrag
Der Käufer hat gegenüber dem Verkäufer keine Verpflichtung, einen Versicherungsvertrag abzuschließen. Allerdings hat der Käufer dem Verkäufer auf dessen Verlangen die für den Abschluss einer Versicherung notwendigen Informationen zur Verfügung zu stellen.

B4 Übernahme

Der Käufer muss die Ware übernehmen, wenn sie wie in **A4** vorgesehen geliefert worden ist.

A5 Gefahrenübergang

Der Verkäufer trägt bis zur Lieferung gemäß **A4** alle Gefahren des Verlustes oder der Beschädigung der Ware, mit Ausnahme von Verlust oder Beschädigung unter den in **B5** beschriebenen Umständen.

A6 Kostenverteilung

Der Verkäufer hat zu tragen

a. zusätzlich zu den aus **A3 a** entstehenden Kosten alle die Ware betreffenden Kosten bis diese gemäß **A4** geliefert worden ist, ausgenommen solcher Kosten, die wie in **B6** vorgesehen vom Käufer zu tragen sind;

b. alle Abgaben für die Entladung am Bestimmungsort, die gemäß Beförderungsvertrag vom Verkäufer zu tragen sind; und

c. falls zutreffend, die Kosten der für die Aus- und Einfuhr notwendigen Zollformalitäten sowie alle Zölle, Steuern und andere Abgaben, die bei der Aus- und Einfuhr der Ware fällig werden, und die Kosten für ihre Durchfuhr durch jedes Land vor Lieferung gemäß **A4**.

A7 Benachrichtigungen an den Käufer

Der Verkäufer hat den Käufer über alles Nötige zu benachrichtigen, damit dieser die üblicherweise notwendigen Maßnahmen zur Übernahme der Ware treffen kann.

B5 Gefahrenübergang

Der Käufer trägt alle Gefahren des Verlustes oder der Beschädigung der Ware ab dem Zeitpunkt, an dem sie wie in **A4** vorgesehen geliefert worden ist.

Falls

a. der Käufer seine Verpflichtungen gemäß **B2** nicht erfüllt, trägt er alle daraus resultierenden Gefahren des Verlustes oder der Beschädigung der Ware; oder

b. der Käufer es unterlässt, gemäß **B7** zu benachrichtigen, trägt er alle Gefahren des Verlustes oder der Beschädigung der Ware ab dem vereinbarten Lieferzeitpunkt oder ab Ablauf des vereinbarten Lieferzeitraums,

vorausgesetzt, die Ware ist eindeutig als die vertragliche Ware kenntlich gemacht worden.

B6 Kostenverteilung

Der Käufer hat zu tragen

a. alle die Ware betreffenden Kosten ab dem Zeitpunkt, an dem sie wie in **A4** vorgesehen geliefert worden ist;

b. alle Entladekosten, die erforderlich sind, um die Ware vom ankommenden Beförderungsmittel am benannten Bestimmungsort zu übernehmen, sofern diese Kosten gemäß Beförderungsvertrag nicht zu Lasten des Verkäufers gehen; und

c. alle zusätzlichen Kosten, die entstehen, falls der Käufer seine Verpflichtungen gemäß **B2** nicht erfüllt, oder es unterlässt, gemäß **B7** zu benachrichtigen, vorausgesetzt, die Ware ist eindeutig als die vertragliche Ware kenntlich gemacht worden.

B7 Benachrichtigungen an den Verkäufer

Wann immer der Käufer berechtigt ist, den Zeitpunkt innerhalb einer vereinbarten Lieferfrist und/oder die Stelle für die Warenübernahme am benannten Bestimmungsort zu bestimmen, hat er den Verkäufer in angemessener Weise darüber zu benachrichtigen.

A8 Transportdokument

Der Verkäufer hat auf eigene Kosten dem Käufer ein Dokument zur Verfügung zu stellen, das diesem die Übernahme der Ware wie in **A4/B4** vorgesehen ermöglicht.

A9 Prüfung – Verpackung – Kennzeichnung

Der Verkäufer hat die Kosten jener Prüfvorgänge (wie Qualitätsprüfung, Messen, Wiegen und Zählen), die notwendig sind, um die Ware gemäß **A4** zu liefern, sowie die Kosten für alle von den Behörden des Aus- oder Einfuhrlandes angeordneten Warenkontrollen vor der Verladung (pre-shipment inspection) zu tragen.

Der Verkäufer hat auf eigene Kosten die Ware zu verpacken, es sei denn, es ist handelsüblich, die jeweilige Art der verkauften Ware unverpackt zu transportieren. Der Verkäufer kann die Ware in der für ihren Transport geeigneten Weise verpacken, es sei denn, der Käufer hat den Verkäufer vor Vertragsschluss über spezifische Verpackungsanforderungen in Kenntnis gesetzt. Die Verpackung ist in geeigneter Weise zu kennzeichnen.

A10 Unterstützung bei Information und damit verbundene Kosten

Der Verkäufer hat, falls zutreffend, dem Käufer auf dessen Verlangen, Gefahr und Kosten rechtzeitig alle Dokumente und Informationen, einschließlich sicherheitsrelevanter Informationen, die der Käufer für den Transport der Ware bis zum endgültigen Bestimmungsort, falls zutreffend, vom benannten Bestimmungsort benötigt, zur Verfügung zu stellen oder ihn bei deren Beschaffung zu unterstützen.

Der Verkäufer hat dem Käufer alle Kosten und Abgaben zu erstatten, die dem Käufer durch das Zurverfügungstellen oder die Unterstützung bei der Beschaffung der in **B10** vorgesehenen Dokumente und Informationen entstanden sind.

B8 Liefernachweis

Der Käufer hat den wie in **A8** vorgesehen zur Verfügung gestellten Liefernachweis anzunehmen.

B9 Prüfung der Ware

Der Käufer hat gegenüber dem Verkäufer keine Verpflichtung, die Kosten für die vor der Verladung zwingend erforderlichen, von den Behörden des Aus- oder Einfuhrlandes angeordneten Warenkontrollen (pre-shipment inspection) zu tragen.

B10 Unterstützung bei Informationen und damit verbundene Kosten

Der Käufer hat dem Verkäufer rechtzeitig alle sicherheitsrelevanten Informationsanforderungen mitzuteilen, so dass der Verkäufer die Verpflichtungen entsprechend **A10** erfüllen kann.

Der Käufer hat dem Verkäufer alle Kosten und Abgaben zu erstatten, die dem Verkäufer durch das Zurverfügungstellen oder die Unterstützung bei der Beschaffung der Dokumente und Informationen wie in **A10** vorgesehen entstanden sind.

Der Käufer hat, falls zutreffend, dem Verkäufer rechtzeitig auf dessen Verlangen, Gefahr und Kosten alle Dokumente und Informationen, einschließlich sicherheitsrelevanter Informationen, die der Verkäufer für Transport, Aus- und Einfuhr der Ware sowie für ihre Durchfuhr durch jedes Land benötigt, zur Verfügung zu stellen oder ihn bei deren Beschaffung zu unterstützen.

KLAUSELN FÜR DEN SEE- UND BINNENSCHIFFS-TRANSPORT

FAS
FREI LÄNGSSEITE SCHIFF

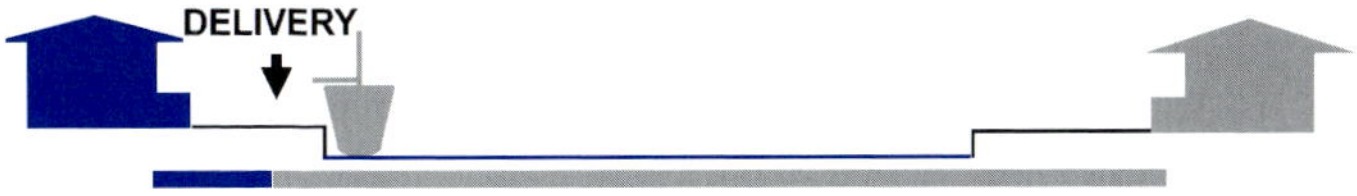

FAS *(fügen Sie den benannten Verschiffungshafen ein)* Incoterms® 2010

ANWENDUNGSHINWEIS

Diese Klausel ist ausschließlich für den See- und Binnenschiffstransport geeignet.

„Frei Längsseite Schiff" bedeutet, dass der Verkäufer liefert, wenn die Ware längsseits des vom Käufer benannten Schiffs (z. B. an einer Kaianlage oder auf einem Binnenschiff) im benannten Verschiffungshafen gebracht ist. Die Gefahr des Verlustes oder der Beschädigung der Ware geht über, wenn sich die Ware längsseits des Schiffs befindet. Der Käufer trägt ab diesem Zeitpunkt alle Kosten.

Die Parteien sind gut beraten, die Ladestelle im benannten Verschiffungshafen so genau wie möglich zu bestimmen, da die Kosten und Gefahren bis zu dieser Stelle zu Lasten des Verkäufers gehen. Diese Kosten und damit verbundene Umschlagskosten (handling charges) können entsprechend der Hafenpraxis variieren.

Der Verkäufer ist verpflichtet, die Ware entweder längsseits des Schiffs zu liefern oder bereits so für die Verschiffung gelieferte Ware zu verschaffen. Der Hinweis „zu verschaffen" bezieht sich hier auf mehrere hintereinander geschaltete Verkäufe in einer Verkaufskette („string sales"), die insbesondere im Rohstoffhandel vorkommen.

Bei containerisierter Ware ist es für den Verkäufer üblich, die Ware nicht längsseits des Schiffs, sondern an den Frachtführer im Terminal zu übergeben. In derartigen Fällen wäre die FAS-Klausel ungeeignet und es sollte die FCA-Klausel verwendet werden.

FAS verpflichtet den Verkäufer, falls zutreffend, die Ware zur Ausfuhr freizumachen. Jedoch hat der Verkäufer keine Verpflichtung, die Ware zur Einfuhr freizumachen, Einfuhrzölle zu zahlen oder Einfuhrzollformalitäten zu erledigen.

A VERPFLICHTUNGEN DES VERKÄUFERS

A1 Allgemeine Verpflichtungen des Verkäufers

Der Verkäufer hat die Ware und die Handelsrechnung in Übereinstimmung mit dem Kaufvertrag bereitzustellen und jeden sonstigen vertraglich vereinbarten Konformitätsnachweis zu erbringen.

Jedes Dokument, auf das in **A1–A10** Bezug genommen wird, kann auch ein entsprechender elektronischer Beleg oder ein entsprechendes elektronisches Verfahren sein, wenn dies zwischen den Parteien vereinbart oder üblich ist.

A2 Lizenzen, Genehmigungen, Sicherheitsfreigaben und andere Formalitäten

Falls zutreffend, hat der Verkäufer auf eigene Gefahr und Kosten die Ausfuhrgenehmigung oder andere behördliche Genehmigungen zu beschaffen sowie alle Zollformalitäten zu erledigen, die für die Ausfuhr der Ware erforderlich sind.

A3 Beförderungs- und Versicherungsverträge

a. Beförderungsvertrag

Der Verkäufer hat gegenüber dem Käufer keine Verpflichtung, einen Beförderungsvertrag abzuschließen. Wenn es der Käufer jedoch verlangt oder es in der Handelspraxis üblich ist und der Käufer keine gegenteilige Anweisung rechtzeitig erteilt, kann der Verkäufer zu üblichen Bedingungen den Beförderungsvertrag auf Gefahr und Kosten des Käufers abschließen. In beiden Fällen kann der Verkäufer es ablehnen, den Beförderungsvertrag abzuschließen, wovon er den Käufer umgehend in Kenntnis zu setzen hat.

b. Versicherungsvertrag

Der Verkäufer hat gegenüber dem Käufer keine Verpflichtung, einen Versicherungsvertrag abzuschließen. Jedoch hat der Verkäufer dem Käufer auf dessen Verlangen, Gefahr und (gegebenenfalls entstehende) Kosten, jene Informationen zur Verfügung zu stellen, die der Käufer für den Abschluss einer Versicherung benötigt.

B VERPFLICHTUNGEN DES KÄUFERS

B1 Allgemeine Verpflichtungen des Käufers

Der Käufer hat den im Kaufvertrag genannten Preis der Ware zu zahlen.

Jedes Dokument, auf das in **B1–B10** Bezug genommen wird, kann auch ein entsprechender elektronischer Beleg oder ein entsprechendes elektronisches Verfahren sein, wenn dies zwischen den Parteien vereinbart oder üblich ist.

B2 Lizenzen, Genehmigungen, Sicherheitsfreigaben und andere Formalitäten

Falls zutreffend, obliegt es dem Käufer, auf eigene Gefahr und Kosten die Einfuhrgenehmigung oder andere behördliche Genehmigungen zu beschaffen sowie alle Zollformalitäten für die Einfuhr der Ware und für ihre Durchfuhr durch jedes Land zu erledigen.

B3 Beförderungs- und Versicherungsverträge

a. Beförderungsvertrag
Der Käufer hat auf eigene Kosten den Vertrag über die Beförderung der Ware vom benannten Verschiffungshafen abzuschließen, sofern der Beförderungsvertrag nicht vom Verkäufer wie in **A3 a** vorgesehen abgeschlossen wurde.

b. Versicherungsvertrag
Der Käufer hat gegenüber dem Verkäufer keine Verpflichtung, einen Versicherungsvertrag abzuschließen.

A4 Lieferung

Der Verkäufer hat die Ware entweder durch Bereitstellung längsseits des vom Käufer benannten Schiffs an der gegebenenfalls vom Käufer benannten Ladestelle im benannten Verschiffungshafen zu liefern oder indem er die so gelieferte Ware verschafft. In beiden Fällen hat der Verkäufer die Ware zum vereinbarten Zeitpunkt oder innerhalb des vereinbarten Zeitraums und in der im Hafen üblichen Weise zu liefern.

Falls keine bestimmte Ladestelle durch den Käufer angegeben worden ist, kann der Verkäufer die für den Zweck am besten geeignete Stelle innerhalb des benannten Verschiffungshafens auswählen. Falls die Parteien vereinbart haben, dass die Lieferung innerhalb eines Zeitraums stattfinden soll, hat der Käufer die Möglichkeit, den Zeitpunkt innerhalb dieser Frist zu wählen.

A5 Gefahrenübergang

Der Verkäufer trägt bis zur Lieferung gemäß **A4** alle Gefahren des Verlustes oder der Beschädigung der Ware, mit Ausnahme von Verlust oder Beschädigung unter den in **B5** beschriebenen Umständen.

B4 Übernahme

Der Käufer muss die Ware übernehmen, wenn sie wie in **A4** vorgesehen geliefert worden ist.

B5 Gefahrenübergang

Der Käufer trägt alle Gefahren des Verlustes oder der Beschädigung der Ware ab dem Zeitpunkt, an dem sie wie in **A4** vorgesehen geliefert worden ist.

Falls

a. der Käufer es unterlässt, gemäß **B7** zu benachrichtigen; oder

b. das vom Käufer benannte Schiff nicht rechtzeitig eintrifft oder die Ware nicht übernimmt oder schon vor dem gemäß **B7** festgesetzten Zeitpunkt keine Ladung mehr annimmt;

dann trägt der Käufer alle Gefahren des Verlustes oder der Beschädigung der Ware ab dem vereinbarten Lieferzeitpunkt oder ab Ablauf des für Lieferung vereinbarten Zeitraums, vorausgesetzt, die Ware ist eindeutig als die vertragliche Ware kenntlich gemacht worden.

A6 Kostenverteilung

Der Verkäufer hat zu tragen

a. alle die Ware betreffenden Kosten bis diese gemäß **A4** geliefert worden ist, ausgenommen solcher Kosten, die wie in **B6** vorgesehen vom Käufer zu tragen sind; und

b. falls zutreffend, die Kosten der für die Ausfuhr notwendigen Zollformalitäten sowie alle Zölle, Steuern und andere Abgaben, die bei der Ausfuhr fällig werden.

A7 Benachrichtigungen an den Käufer

Der Verkäufer hat den Käufer, auf dessen Gefahr und Kosten, in angemessener Weise darüber zu benachrichtigen, entweder, dass die Ware gemäß **A4** geliefert worden ist oder dass das Schiff die Ware nicht innerhalb der vereinbarten Frist geladen hat.

A8 Transportdokument

Der Verkäufer hat auf eigene Kosten dem Käufer den üblichen Nachweis zu erbringen, dass die Ware gemäß **A4** geliefert worden ist.

Sofern es sich bei einem solchen Nachweis nicht um ein Transportdokument handelt, hat der Verkäufer den Käufer auf dessen Verlangen, Gefahr und Kosten bei der Beschaffung eines Transportdokuments zu unterstützen.

B6 Kostenverteilung

Der Käufer hat zu tragen

a. alle die Ware betreffenden Kosten ab dem Zeitpunkt, an dem sie wie in **A4** vorgesehen geliefert worden ist, ausgenommen, falls zutreffend, die Kosten der für die Ausfuhr notwendigen Zollformalitäten sowie alle Zölle, Steuern und andere in **A6 b** genannte Abgaben, die bei der Ausfuhr fällig werden;

b. alle zusätzlichen Kosten, die entweder dadurch entstehen, dass:
   i. der Käufer die angemessene Benachrichtigung gemäß **B7** unterlässt, oder
   ii. das vom Käufer benannte Schiff nicht rechtzeitig eintrifft, die Ware nicht übernehmen kann oder schon vor der gemäß **B7** mitgeteilten Lieferzeit keine Ladung mehr annimmt,

   vorausgesetzt, die Ware ist eindeutig als die vertragliche Ware kenntlich gemacht worden; und

c. falls zutreffend, alle Zölle, Steuern und andere Abgaben sowie Kosten der Zollformalitäten, die bei der Einfuhr der Ware fällig werden, sowie die Kosten für ihre Durchfuhr durch jedes Land.

B7 Benachrichtigungen an den Verkäufer

Der Käufer hat dem Verkäufer in angemessener Weise den Namen des Schiffs, die Ladestelle und, falls erforderlich, die gewählte Lieferzeit innerhalb des vereinbarten Zeitraums anzugeben.

B8 Liefernachweis

Der Käufer hat den wie in **A8** vorgesehen zur Verfügung gestellten Liefernachweis anzunehmen.

A9 Prüfung – Verpackung – Kennzeichnung

Der Verkäufer hat die Kosten jener Prüfvorgänge (wie Qualitätsprüfung, Messen, Wiegen und Zählen), die notwendig sind, um die Ware gemäß **A4** zu liefern, sowie die Kosten für alle von den Behörden des Ausfuhrlandes angeordneten Warenkontrollen vor der Verladung (pre-shipment inspection) zu tragen.

Der Verkäufer hat auf eigene Kosten die Ware zu verpacken, sofern es nicht handelsüblich ist, die jeweilige Art der verkauften Ware unverpackt zu transportieren. Der Verkäufer kann die Ware in der Weise verpacken, die für ihren Transport angemessen ist, es sei denn, der Käufer hat den Verkäufer über spezifische Verpackungsanforderungen vor Vertragsschluss in Kenntnis gesetzt. Die Verpackung ist in geeigneter Weise zu kennzeichnen.

A10 Unterstützung bei Informationen und damit verbundene Kosten

Der Verkäufer hat, falls zutreffend, dem Käufer auf dessen Verlangen, Gefahr und Kosten rechtzeitig alle Dokumente und Informationen, einschließlich sicherheitsrelevanter Informationen, die der Käufer für die Einfuhr der Ware und/oder für ihren Transport bis zum endgültigen Bestimmungsort benötigt, zur Verfügung zu stellen oder ihn bei deren Beschaffung zu unterstützen.

Der Verkäufer hat dem Käufer alle Kosten und Abgaben zu erstatten, die dem Käufer durch das Zurverfügungstellen oder die Unterstützung bei der Beschaffung der in **B10** vorgesehenen Dokumente und Informationen entstanden sind.

B9 Prüfung der Ware

Der Käufer hat die Kosten für jede vor der Verladung zwingend erforderliche Warenkontrolle (pre-shipment inspection) zu tragen, mit Ausnahme behördlich angeordneter Kontrollen des Ausfuhrlandes.

B10 Unterstützung bei Informationen und damit verbundene Kosten

Der Käufer hat dem Verkäufer rechtzeitig alle sicherheitsrelevanten Informationsanforderungen mitzuteilen, so dass der Verkäufer die Verpflichtungen entsprechend **A10** erfüllen kann.

Der Käufer hat dem Verkäufer alle Kosten und Abgaben zu erstatten, die dem Verkäufer durch das Zurverfügungstellen oder die Unterstützung bei der Beschaffung der Dokumente und Informationen wie in **A10** vorgesehen entstanden sind.

Der Käufer hat, falls zutreffend, dem Verkäufer rechtzeitig auf dessen Verlangen, Gefahr und Kosten alle Dokumente und Informationen, einschließlich sicherheitsrelevanter Informationen, die der Verkäufer für den Transport und die Ausfuhr der Ware sowie für ihre Durchfuhr durch jedes Land benötigt, zur Verfügung zu stellen oder ihn bei deren Beschaffung zu unterstützen.

FOB
FREI AN BORD

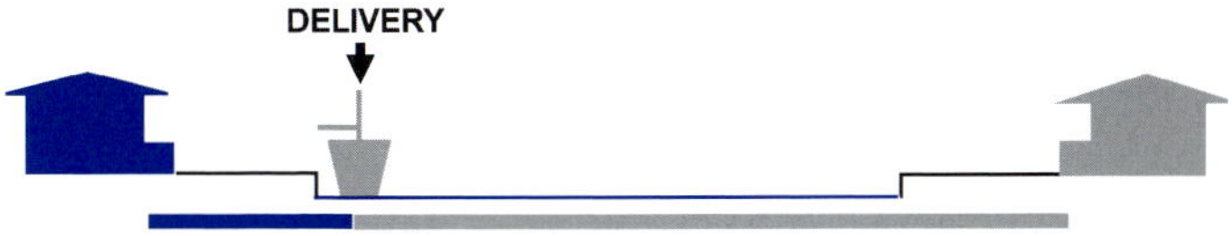

FOB *(fügen Sie den benannten Verschiffungshafen ein)* Incoterms® 2010

ANWENDUNGSHINWEIS

Diese Klausel ist ausschließlich für den See- und Binnenschiffstransport geeignet.

„Frei an Bord" bedeutet, dass der Verkäufer die Ware an Bord des vom Käufer benannten Schiffs im benannten Verschiffungshafen liefert oder die bereits so gelieferte Ware verschafft. Die Gefahr des Verlustes oder der Beschädigung der Ware geht über, wenn die Ware an Bord des Schiffs ist. Der Käufer trägt ab diesem Zeitpunkt alle Kosten.

Der Verkäufer ist verpflichtet, die Ware entweder an Bord des Schiffs zu liefern oder bereits so für die Verschiffung gelieferte Ware zu verschaffen. Der Hinweis „zu verschaffen" bezieht sich hier auf mehrere hintereinander geschaltete Verkäufe in einer Verkaufskette („string sales"), die insbesondere im Rohstoffhandel vorkommen.

FOB kann ungeeignet sein, wenn die Ware dem Frachtführer übergeben wird, bevor sie sich auf dem Schiff befindet, z. B. bei containerisierter Ware, welche üblicherweise am Terminal geliefert wird. In derartigen Fällen sollte die FCA-Klausel verwendet werden.

FOB verpflichtet den Verkäufer, falls zutreffend, die Ware zur Ausfuhr freizumachen. Jedoch hat der Verkäufer keine Verpflichtung, die Ware zur Einfuhr freizumachen, Einfuhrzölle zu zahlen oder Einfuhrzollformalitäten zu erledigen.

A VERPFLICHTUNGEN DES VERKÄUFERS

A1 Allgemeine Verpflichtungen des Verkäufers

Der Verkäufer hat die Ware und die Handelsrechnung in Übereinstimmung mit dem Kaufvertrag bereitzustellen und jeden sonstigen vertraglich vereinbarten Konformitätsnachweis zu erbringen.

Jedes Dokument, auf das in **A1–A10** Bezug genommen wird, kann auch ein entsprechender elektronischer Beleg oder ein entsprechendes elektronisches Verfahren sein, wenn dies zwischen den Parteien vereinbart oder üblich ist.

A2 Lizenzen, Genehmigungen, Sicherheitsfreigaben und andere Formalitäten

Falls zutreffend, hat der Verkäufer auf eigene Gefahr und Kosten die Ausfuhrgenehmigung oder andere behördliche Genehmigungen zu beschaffen sowie alle Zollformalitäten zu erledigen, die für die Ausfuhr der Ware erforderlich sind.

A3 Beförderungs- und Versicherungsverträge

a. Beförderungsvertrag

Der Verkäufer hat gegenüber dem Käufer keine Verpflichtung, einen Beförderungsvertrag abzuschließen. Wenn es der Käufer jedoch verlangt oder es in der Handelspraxis üblich ist und der Käufer keine gegenteilige Anweisung rechtzeitig erteilt, kann der Verkäufer zu üblichen Bedingungen den Beförderungsvertrag auf Gefahr und Kosten des Käufers abschließen. In beiden Fällen kann der Verkäufer es ablehnen, den Beförderungsvertrag abzuschließen, wovon er den Käufer umgehend in Kenntnis zu setzen hat.

b. Versicherungsvertrag

Der Verkäufer hat gegenüber dem Käufer keine Verpflichtung, einen Versicherungsvertrag abzuschließen. Jedoch hat der Verkäufer dem Käufer auf dessen Verlangen, Gefahr und (gegebenenfalls entstehende) Kosten, jene Informationen zur Verfügung zu stellen, die der Käufer für den Abschluss einer Versicherung benötigt.

B VERPFLICHTUNGEN DES KÄUFERS

B1 Allgemeine Verpflichtungen des Käufers

Der Käufer hat den im Kaufvertrag genannten Preis der Ware zu zahlen.

Jedes Dokument, auf das in **B1–B10** Bezug genommen wird, kann auch ein entsprechender elektronischer Beleg oder ein entsprechendes elektronisches Verfahren sein, wenn dies zwischen den Parteien vereinbart oder üblich ist.

B2 Lizenzen, Genehmigungen, Sicherheitsfreigaben und andere Formalitäten

Falls zutreffend, obliegt es dem Käufer, auf eigene Gefahr und Kosten die Einfuhrgenehmigung oder andere behördliche Genehmigungen zu beschaffen sowie alle Zollformalitäten für die Einfuhr der Ware und für ihre Durchfuhr durch jedes Land zu erledigen.

B3 Beförderungs- und Versicherungsverträge

a. Beförderungsvertrag
Der Käufer hat auf eigene Kosten den Vertrag über die Beförderung der Ware vom benannten Verschiffungshafen abzuschließen, sofern der Beförderungsvertrag nicht vom Verkäufer wie in **A3a** vorgesehen abgeschlossen wurde.

b. Versicherungsvertrag
Der Käufer hat gegenüber dem Verkäufer keine Verpflichtung, einen Versicherungsvertrag abzuschließen.

A4 Lieferung

Der Verkäufer hat die Ware zu liefern, entweder, indem er sie an Bord des vom Käufer benannten Schiffs an der gegebenenfalls vom Käufer bestimmten Ladestelle im benannten Verschiffungshafen verbringt oder indem er die so gelieferte Ware verschafft. In beiden Fällen hat der Verkäufer die Ware zum vereinbarten Zeitpunkt oder innerhalb des vereinbarten Zeitraums und in der im Hafen üblichen Weise zu liefern.

Falls keine bestimmte Ladestelle durch den Käufer angegeben worden ist, kann der Verkäufer die für den Zweck am besten geeignete Stelle innerhalb des benannten Verschiffungshafens auswählen.

A5 Gefahrenübergang

Der Verkäufer trägt bis zur Lieferung gemäß **A4** alle Gefahren des Verlustes oder der Beschädigung der Ware, mit Ausnahme von Verlust oder Beschädigung unter den in **B5** beschriebenen Umständen.

B4 Übernahme

Der Käufer muss die Ware übernehmen, wenn sie wie in **A4** vorgesehen geliefert worden ist.

B5 Gefahrenübergang

Der Käufer trägt alle Gefahren des Verlustes oder der Beschädigung der Ware ab dem Zeitpunkt, an dem sie wie in **A4** vorgesehen geliefert worden ist.

Falls

a. der Käufer die Benachrichtigung gemäß **B7** über die Benennung eines Schiffs unterlässt; oder

b. das vom Käufer benannte Schiff nicht rechtzeitig eintrifft, um es dem Verkäufer zu ermöglichen, seine Pflichten entsprechend **A4** zu erfüllen, es die Ware nicht übernehmen kann oder schon vor dem gemäß **B7** festgesetzten Zeitpunkt keine Ladung mehr annimmt;

dann trägt der Käufer alle Gefahren des Verlustes oder der Beschädigung der Ware:

i. ab dem vereinbarten Zeitpunkt, oder mangels eines vereinbarten Zeitpunkts,

ii. ab dem vom Verkäufer gemäß **A7** mitgeteilten Zeitpunkt innerhalb des vereinbarten Zeitraums oder, falls kein solcher Zeitpunkt mitgeteilt wurde,

iii. ab dem Ablaufdatum eines vereinbarten Lieferzeitraums,

vorausgesetzt, die Ware ist eindeutig als die vertragliche Ware kenntlich gemacht worden.

A6 Kostenverteilung

Der Verkäufer hat zu tragen

a. alle die Ware betreffenden Kosten bis diese gemäß **A4** geliefert worden ist, ausgenommen solcher Kosten, die wie in **B6** vorgesehen vom Käufer zu tragen sind; und

b. falls zutreffend, die Kosten der für die Ausfuhr notwendigen Zollformalitäten sowie alle Zölle, Steuern und andere Abgaben, die bei der Ausfuhr fällig werden.

A7 Benachrichtigungen an den Käufer

Der Verkäufer hat den Käufer, auf dessen Gefahr und Kosten, in angemessener Weise darüber zu benachrichtigen, entweder, dass die Ware gemäß **A4** geliefert worden ist oder dass das Schiff die Ware nicht innerhalb der vereinbarten Frist geladen hat.

A8 Transportdokument

Der Verkäufer hat auf eigene Kosten dem Käufer den üblichen Nachweis zu erbringen, dass die Ware gemäß **A4** geliefert worden ist.

Sofern es sich bei einem solchen Nachweis nicht um ein Transportdokument handelt, hat der Verkäufer den Käufer auf dessen Verlangen, Gefahr und Kosten bei der Beschaffung eines Transportdokuments zu unterstützen.

B6 Kostenverteilung

Der Käufer hat zu tragen

a. alle die Ware betreffenden Kosten ab dem Zeitpunkt, an dem sie wie in **A4** vorgesehen geliefert worden ist, ausgenommen, falls zutreffend, die Kosten der für die Ausfuhr notwendigen Zollformalitäten sowie alle Zölle, Steuern und andere in **A6 b** genannte Abgaben, die bei der Ausfuhr fällig werden;

b. alle zusätzlichen Kosten, die entweder dadurch entstehen, dass:
   i. der Käufer die angemessene Benachrichtigung gemäß **B7** unterlässt, oder
   ii. das vom Käufer benannte Schiff nicht rechtzeitig eintrifft, die Ware nicht übernehmen kann oder schon vor der gemäß **B7** mitgeteilten Lieferzeit keine Ladung mehr annimmt,

   vorausgesetzt, die Ware ist eindeutig als die vertragliche Ware kenntlich gemacht worden; und

c. falls zutreffend, alle Zölle, Steuern und andere Abgaben sowie die Kosten der Zollformalitäten, die bei der Einfuhr der Ware sowie ihrer Durchfuhr durch jedes Land fällig werden.

B7 Benachrichtigungen an den Verkäufer

Der Käufer hat dem Verkäufer in angemessener Weise den Namen des Schiffs, die Ladestelle und, falls erforderlich, die gewählte Lieferzeit innerhalb des vereinbarten Lieferzeitraums anzugeben.

B8 Liefernachweis

Der Käufer hat den wie in **A8** vorgesehen zur Verfügung gestellten Liefernachweis anzunehmen.

A9 Prüfung – Verpackung – Kennzeichnung

Der Verkäufer hat die Kosten jener Prüfvorgänge (wie Qualitätsprüfung, Messen, Wiegen und Zählen), die notwendig sind, um die Ware gemäß **A4** zu liefern, sowie die Kosten für alle von den Behörden des Ausfuhrlandes angeordneten Warenkontrollen vor der Verladung (pre-shipment inspection) zu tragen.

Der Verkäufer hat auf eigene Kosten die Ware zu verpacken, sofern es nicht handelsüblich ist, die jeweilige Art der verkauften Ware unverpackt zu transportieren. Der Verkäufer kann die Ware in der Weise verpacken, die für ihren Transport angemessen ist, es sei denn, der Käufer hat den Verkäufer über spezifische Verpackungsanforderungen vor Vertragsschluss in Kenntnis gesetzt. Die Verpackung ist in geeigneter Weise zu kennzeichnen.

A10 Unterstützung bei Informationen und damit verbundene Kosten

Der Verkäufer hat, falls zutreffend, dem Käufer auf dessen Verlangen, Gefahr und Kosten rechtzeitig alle Dokumente und Informationen, einschließlich sicherheitsrelevanter Informationen, die der Käufer für die Einfuhr der Ware und/oder für ihren Transport bis zum endgültigen Bestimmungsort benötigt, zur Verfügung zu stellen oder ihn bei deren Beschaffung zu unterstützen.

Der Verkäufer hat dem Käufer alle Kosten und Abgaben zu erstatten, die dem Käufer durch das Zurverfügungstellen oder die Unterstützung bei der Beschaffung der in **B10** vorgesehenen Dokumente und Informationen entstanden sind.

B9 Prüfung der Ware

Der Käufer hat die Kosten für jede vor der Verladung zwingend erforderliche Warenkontrolle (pre-shipment inspection) zu tragen, mit Ausnahme behördlich angeordneter Kontrollen des Ausfuhrlandes.

B10 Unterstützung bei Informationen und damit verbundene Kosten

Der Käufer hat dem Verkäufer rechtzeitig alle sicherheitsrelevanten Informationsanforderungen mitzuteilen, so dass der Verkäufer die Verpflichtungen entsprechend **A10** erfüllen kann.

Der Käufer hat dem Verkäufer alle Kosten und Abgaben zu erstatten, die dem Verkäufer durch das Zurverfügungstellen oder die Unterstützung bei der Beschaffung der Dokumente und Informationen wie in **A10** vorgesehen entstanden sind.

Der Käufer hat, falls zutreffend, dem Verkäufer rechtzeitig auf dessen Verlangen, Gefahr und Kosten alle Dokumente und Informationen, einschließlich sicherheitsrelevanter Informationen, die der Verkäufer für den Transport und die Ausfuhr der Ware sowie für ihre Durchfuhr durch jedes Land benötigt, zur Verfügung zu stellen oder ihn bei deren Beschaffung zu unterstützen.

CFR
KOSTEN UND FRACHT

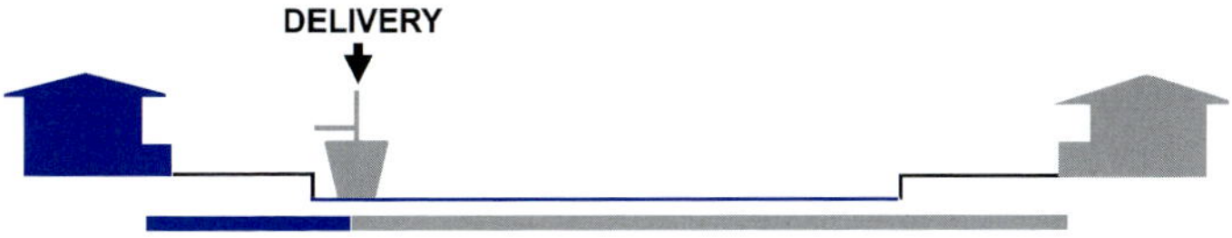

CFR *(fügen Sie den benannten Bestimmungshafen ein)* Incoterms® 2010

ANWENDUNGSHINWEIS

Diese Klausel ist ausschließlich für den See- und Binnenschiffstransport geeignet.

„Kosten und Fracht" bedeutet, dass der Verkäufer die Ware an Bord des Schiffs liefert oder die bereits so gelieferte Ware verschafft. Die Gefahr des Verlustes oder der Beschädigung der Ware geht über, wenn die Ware an Bord des Schiffs ist. Der Verkäufer hat den Beförderungsvertrag abzuschließen und die Kosten und Fracht zu tragen, die für die Beförderung der Ware zum benannten Bestimmungshafen erforderlich sind.

Werden die Klauseln CPT, CIP, CFR oder CIF verwendet, erfüllt der Verkäufer seine Lieferpflicht, wenn er die Ware dem Frachtführer in der gemäß der gewählten Klausel bestimmten Weise übergibt und nicht, wenn die Ware den Bestimmungsort erreicht.

Diese Klausel beinhaltet zwei kritische Punkte, da Gefahren- und Kostenübergang an verschiedenen Orten stattfinden. Während der Vertrag in jedem Fall einen Bestimmungshafen angibt, muss er nicht den Verschiffungshafen angeben. Dort allerdings geht die Gefahr auf den Käufer über. Falls der Verschiffungshafen für den Käufer von besonderer Bedeutung ist, sind die Parteien gut beraten, diesen im Vertrag so genau wie möglich zu bezeichnen.

Die Parteien sind gut beraten, die Stelle im vereinbarten Bestimmungshafen so genau wie möglich zu bezeichnen, da die Kosten bis zu dieser Stelle zu Lasten des Verkäufers gehen. Dem Verkäufer wird geraten, mit dieser Wahl genau übereinstimmende Beförderungsverträge zu verschaffen. Entstehen dem Verkäufer nach seinem Beförderungsvertrag Kosten im Zusammenhang mit der Entladung an der bestimmten Stelle im Bestimmungshafen, dann ist der Verkäufer nicht berechtigt, diese Kosten vom Käufer zurückzufordern, sofern nichts anderes zwischen den Parteien vereinbart ist.

Der Verkäufer ist verpflichtet, die Ware entweder an Bord des Schiffs zu liefern oder bereits so für die Verschiffung an den Bestimmungsort gelieferte Ware zu verschaffen. Zusätzlich ist der Verkäufer verpflichtet, entweder einen Beförderungsvertrag abzuschließen oder einen solchen Vertrag zu verschaffen. Der Hinweis „zu verschaffen" bezieht sich hier auf mehrere hintereinander geschaltete Verkäufe in einer Verkaufskette („string sales"), die insbesondere im Rohstoffhandel vorkommen.

CFR kann ungeeignet sein, wenn die Ware dem Frachtführer übergeben wird, bevor sie sich auf dem Schiff befindet, z. B. bei containerisierter Ware, welche üblicherweise am Terminal geliefert wird. In derartigen Fällen sollte die CPT-Klausel verwendet werden.

CFR verpflichtet den Verkäufer, falls zutreffend, die Ware zur Ausfuhr freizumachen. Jedoch hat der Verkäufer keine Verpflichtung, die Ware zur Einfuhr freizumachen, Einfuhrzölle zu zahlen oder Einfuhrzollformalitäten zu erledigen.

A VERPFLICHTUNGEN DES VERKÄUFERS

A1 Allgemeine Verpflichtungen des Verkäufers

Der Verkäufer hat die Ware und die Handelsrechnung in Übereinstimmung mit dem Kaufvertrag bereitzustellen und jeden sonstigen vertraglich vereinbarten Konformitätsnachweis zu erbringen.

Jedes Dokument, auf das in **A1–A10** Bezug genommen wird, kann auch ein entsprechender elektronischer Beleg oder ein entsprechendes elektronisches Verfahren sein, wenn dies zwischen den Parteien vereinbart oder üblich ist.

A2 Lizenzen, Genehmigungen, Sicherheitsfreigaben und andere Formalitäten

Falls zutreffend, hat der Verkäufer auf eigene Gefahr und Kosten die Ausfuhrgenehmigung oder andere behördliche Genehmigungen zu beschaffen sowie alle Zollformalitäten zu erledigen, die für die Ausfuhr der Ware erforderlich sind.

A3 Beförderungs- und Versicherungsverträge

a. Beförderungsvertrag
Der Verkäufer muss einen Vertrag über die Beförderung der Ware von der gegebenenfalls vereinbarten Lieferstelle am Lieferort bis zum benannten Bestimmungshafen oder einer gegebenenfalls vereinbarten Stelle in diesem Hafen abschließen oder verschaffen. Der Beförderungsvertrag muss zu den üblichen Bedingungen auf Kosten des Verkäufers abgeschlossen werden und die Beförderung auf der üblichen Route mit einem Schiff der Bauart gewährleisten, die normalerweise für den Transport der verkauften Warenart verwendet wird.

b. Versicherungsvertrag
Der Verkäufer hat gegenüber dem Käufer keine Verpflichtung, einen Versicherungsvertrag abzuschließen. Jedoch hat der Verkäufer dem Käufer auf dessen Verlangen, Gefahr und (gegebenenfalls entstehende) Kosten jene Informationen zur Verfügung zu stellen, die der Käufer für den Abschluss einer Versicherung benötigt.

B VERPFLICHTUNGEN DES KÄUFERS

B1 Allgemeine Verpflichtungen des Käufers

Der Käufer hat den im Kaufvertrag genannten Preis der Ware zu zahlen.

Jedes Dokument, auf das in **B1–B10** Bezug genommen wird, kann auch ein entsprechender elektronischer Beleg oder ein entsprechendes elektronisches Verfahren sein, wenn dies zwischen den Parteien vereinbart oder üblich ist.

B2 Lizenzen, Genehmigungen, Sicherheitsfreigaben und andere Formalitäten

Falls zutreffend, obliegt es dem Käufer, auf eigene Gefahr und Kosten die Einfuhrgenehmigung oder andere behördliche Genehmigungen zu beschaffen sowie alle Zollformalitäten für die Einfuhr der Ware und für ihre Durchfuhr durch jedes Land zu erledigen.

B3 Beförderungs- und Versicherungsverträge

a. Beförderungsvertrag
Der Käufer hat gegenüber dem Verkäufer keine Verpflichtung, einen Beförderungsvertrag abzuschließen.

b. Versicherungsvertrag
Der Käufer hat gegenüber dem Verkäufer keine Verpflichtung, einen Versicherungsvertrag abzuschließen. Allerdings hat der Käufer dem Verkäufer auf dessen Verlangen die notwendigen Informationen für den Abschluss einer Versicherung zur Verfügung zu stellen.

A4 Lieferung

Der Verkäufer hat die Ware zu liefern, entweder, indem er sie an Bord des Schiffs verbringt oder indem er die so gelieferte Ware verschafft. In beiden Fällen hat der Verkäufer die Ware zum vereinbarten Zeitpunkt oder innerhalb des vereinbarten Zeitraums und in der im Hafen üblichen Weise zu liefern.

A5 Gefahrenübergang

Der Verkäufer trägt bis zur Lieferung gemäß **A4** alle Gefahren des Verlustes oder der Beschädigung der Ware, mit Ausnahme von Verlust oder Beschädigung unter den in **B5** beschriebenen Umständen.

A6 Kostenverteilung

Der Verkäufer hat zu tragen

a. alle die Ware betreffenden Kosten bis diese gemäß **A4** geliefert worden ist, ausgenommen solcher Kosten, die wie in **B6** vorgesehen vom Käufer zu tragen sind;

b. die Fracht und alle anderen aus **A3 a** entstehenden Kosten einschließlich der Kosten für die Verladung der Ware an Bord und aller Entladekosten im vereinbarten Entladehafen, die nach dem Beförderungsvertrag vom Verkäufer zu tragen sind; und

c. falls zutreffend, die Kosten der für die Ausfuhr notwendigen Zollformalitäten sowie alle Zölle, Steuern und andere Abgaben, die bei der Ausfuhr fällig werden, und die Kosten für die Durchfuhr der Ware durch jedes Land, soweit diese nach dem Beförderungsvertrag vom Verkäufer zu tragen sind.

B4 Übernahme

Der Käufer muss die Ware übernehmen, wenn sie wie in **A4** vorgesehen geliefert worden ist, und sie von dem Frachtführer im benannten Bestimmungshafen entgegennehmen.

B5 Gefahrenübergang

Der Käufer trägt alle Gefahren des Verlustes oder der Beschädigung der Ware ab dem Zeitpunkt, an dem sie wie in **A4** vorgesehen geliefert worden ist.

Falls der Käufer es unterlässt, gemäß **B7** zu benachrichtigen, trägt er alle Gefahren des Verlustes oder der Beschädigung der Ware ab dem für die Verschiffung vereinbarten Zeitpunkt oder ab Ablauf der hierfür vereinbarten Frist, vorausgesetzt, die Ware ist eindeutig als die vertragliche Ware kenntlich gemacht worden.

B6 Kostenverteilung

Der Käufer hat, vorbehaltlich der Bestimmungen in **A3 a**, zu tragen

a. alle die Ware betreffenden Kosten ab dem Zeitpunkt, an dem sie wie in **A4** vorgesehen geliefert worden ist, ausgenommen, falls zutreffend, die Kosten der für die Ausfuhr notwendigen Zollformalitäten sowie alle Zölle, Steuern und andere in **A6 c** genannte Abgaben, die bei der Ausfuhr fällig werden;

b. alle die Ware betreffenden Kosten und Abgaben während des Transports bis zu ihrer Ankunft im Bestimmungshafen, es sei denn, solche Kosten und Abgaben gehen gemäß dem Beförderungsvertrag zu Lasten des Verkäufers;

c. die Entladekosten, einschließlich Kosten für Leichterung und Kaigebühren, es sei denn, diese Kosten und Abgaben sind nach dem Beförderungsvertrag vom Verkäufer zu tragen;

d. alle zusätzlichen Kosten, die entstehen, sollte er die Benachrichtigung gemäß **B7** unterlassen, ab dem für die Verschiffung vereinbarten Zeitpunkt oder ab Ablauf der

A7 Benachrichtigungen an den Käufer

Der Verkäufer hat den Käufer über alles Nötige zu benachrichtigen, damit dieser die üblicherweise notwendigen Maßnahmen zur Übernahme der Ware treffen kann.

A8 Transportdokument

Der Verkäufer hat auf eigene Kosten dem Käufer unverzüglich das übliche Transportdokument für den vereinbarten Bestimmungshafen zur Verfügung zu stellen.

Dieses Transportdokument muss über die vertragliche Ware lauten, ein innerhalb der für die Verschiffung vereinbarten Frist liegendes Datum tragen, den Käufer berechtigen, die Herausgabe der Ware im Bestimmungshafen von dem Frachtführer zu verlangen und, sofern nichts anderes vereinbart wurde, es dem Käufer ermöglichen, die Ware während des Transports an einen nachfolgenden Käufer durch Übertragung des Dokuments oder durch Mitteilung an den Frachtführer zu verkaufen.

Wird ein solches Transportdokument als begebbares Dokument und in mehreren Originalen ausgestellt, muss ein vollständiger Satz von Originalen dem Käufer übergeben werden.

hierfür vereinbarten Frist, vorausgesetzt, die Ware ist eindeutig als die vertragliche Ware kenntlich gemacht worden; und

e. falls zutreffend, alle Zölle, Steuern und andere Abgaben sowie die Kosten der Zollformalitäten, die bei der Einfuhr der Ware und, soweit nicht im Beförderungsvertrag enthalten, bei ihrer Durchfuhr durch jedes Land anfallen.

B7 Benachrichtigungen an den Verkäufer

Wann immer der Käufer berechtigt ist, den Zeitpunkt für die Verschiffung der Ware und/oder die Stelle für die Entgegennahme der Ware innerhalb des benannten Bestimmungshafens zu bestimmen, hat er den Verkäufer in angemessener Weise darüber zu benachrichtigen.

B8 Liefernachweis

Der Käufer hat das wie in **A8** vorgesehen zur Verfügung gestellte Transportdokument anzunehmen, wenn dieses mit dem Vertrag übereinstimmt.

A9 Prüfung – Verpackung – Kennzeichnung

Der Verkäufer hat die Kosten jener Prüfvorgänge (wie Qualitätsprüfung, Messen, Wiegen und Zählen), die notwendig sind, um die Ware gemäß **A4** zu liefern, sowie die Kosten für alle von den Behörden des Ausfuhrlandes angeordneten Warenkontrollen vor der Verladung (pre-shipment inspection) zu tragen.

Der Verkäufer hat auf eigene Kosten die Ware zu verpacken, sofern es nicht handelsüblich ist, die jeweilige Art der verkauften Ware unverpackt zu transportieren. Der Verkäufer kann die Ware in der Weise verpacken, die für ihren Transport angemessen ist, es sei denn, der Käufer hat den Verkäufer über spezifische Verpackungsanforderungen vor Vertragsschluss in Kenntnis gesetzt. Die Verpackung ist in geeigneter Weise zu kennzeichnen.

A10 Unterstützung bei Informationen und damit verbundene Kosten

Der Verkäufer hat, falls zutreffend, dem Käufer auf dessen Verlangen, Gefahr und Kosten rechtzeitig alle Dokumente und Informationen, einschließlich sicherheitsrelevanter Informationen, die der Käufer für die Einfuhr der Ware und/oder für ihren Transport bis zum endgültigen Bestimmungsort benötigt, zur Verfügung zu stellen oder ihn bei deren Beschaffung zu unterstützen.

Der Verkäufer hat dem Käufer alle Kosten und Abgaben zu erstatten, die dem Käufer durch das Zurverfügungstellen oder die Unterstützung bei der Beschaffung der in **B10** vorgesehenen Dokumente und Informationen entstanden sind.

B9 Prüfung der Ware

Der Käufer hat die Kosten für jede vor der Verladung zwingend erforderliche Warenkontrolle (pre-shipment inspection) zu tragen, mit Ausnahme behördlich angeordneter Kontrollen des Ausfuhrlandes.

B10 Unterstützung bei Informationen und damit verbundene Kosten

Der Käufer hat dem Verkäufer rechtzeitig alle sicherheitsrelevanten Informationsanforderungen mitzuteilen, so dass der Verkäufer die Verpflichtungen entsprechend **A10** erfüllen kann.

Der Käufer hat dem Verkäufer alle Kosten und Abgaben zu erstatten, die dem Verkäufer durch das Zurverfügungstellen oder die Unterstützung bei der Beschaffung der Dokumente und Informationen wie in **A10** vorgesehen entstanden sind.

Der Käufer hat, falls zutreffend, dem Verkäufer rechtzeitig auf dessen Verlangen, Gefahr und Kosten alle Dokumente und Informationen, einschließlich sicherheitsrelevanter Informationen, die der Verkäufer für den Transport und die Ausfuhr der Ware sowie für ihre Durchfuhr durch jedes Land benötigt, zur Verfügung zu stellen oder ihn bei deren Beschaffung zu unterstützen.

CIF

KOSTEN, VERSICHERUNG UND FRACHT

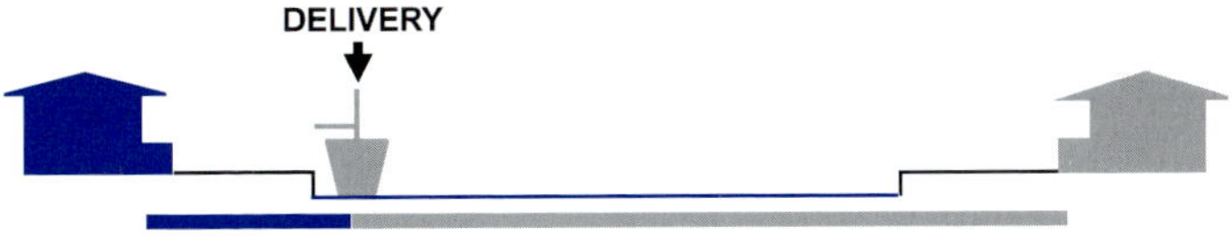

CIF *(fügen Sie den benannten Bestimmungshafen ein)* Incoterms® 2010

ANWENDUNGSHINWEIS

Diese Klausel ist ausschließlich für den See- und Binnenschiffstransport geeignet.

„Kosten, Versicherung und Fracht" bedeutet, dass der Verkäufer die Ware an Bord des Schiffs liefert oder die bereits so gelieferte Ware verschafft. Die Gefahr des Verlustes oder der Beschädigung der Ware geht über, wenn die Ware an Bord des Schiffs ist. Der Verkäufer hat den Beförderungsvertrag abzuschließen sowie die Kosten und Fracht zu tragen, die für die Beförderung der Ware zum benannten Bestimmungshafen erforderlich sind.

Der Verkäufer schließt auch einen Versicherungsvertrag gegen die vom Käufer getragene Gefahr des Verlustes oder der Beschädigung der Ware während des Transports ab. Der Käufer sollte beachten, dass gemäß der CIF-Klausel der Verkäufer nur verpflichtet ist, eine Versicherung mit Mindestdeckung abzuschließen. Wünscht der Käufer einen höheren Versicherungsschutz, wird er dies entweder ausdrücklich mit dem Verkäufer vereinbaren oder eigene zusätzliche Versicherungsvorkehrungen treffen müssen.

Werden die Klauseln CPT, CIP, CFR oder CIF verwendet, erfüllt der Verkäufer seine Lieferpflicht, sobald er die Ware dem Frachtführer in der nach der gewählten Klausel bestimmten Weise übergibt und nicht, wenn die Ware den Bestimmungsort erreicht.

Diese Klausel beinhaltet zwei kritische Punkte, da Gefahren- und Kostenübergang an verschiedenen Orten stattfinden. Während der Vertrag in jedem Fall den Bestimmungshafen angibt, muss er nicht den Verschiffungshafen angeben. Dort allerdings geht die Gefahr auf den Käufer über. Falls der Verschiffungshafen für den Käufer von besonderer Bedeutung ist, sind die Parteien gut beraten, diesen im Vertrag so genau wie möglich zu bezeichnen.

Die Parteien sind gut beraten, die Stelle im vereinbarten Bestimmungshafen so genau wie möglich zu bezeichnen, da die Kosten bis zu dieser Stelle zu Lasten des Verkäufers gehen. Dem Verkäufer wird geraten, mit dieser Wahl genau übereinstimmende Beförderungsverträge zu verschaffen. Entstehen dem Verkäufer nach seinem Beförderungsvertrag Kosten im Zusammenhang mit der Entladung an der bestimmten Stelle im Bestimmungshafen, dann ist der Verkäufer nicht berechtigt, diese Kosten vom Käufer zurückzufordern, sofern nichts anderes zwischen den Parteien vereinbart ist.

Der Verkäufer ist verpflichtet, die Ware entweder an Bord des Schiffs zu liefern oder bereits so für die Verschiffung an den Bestimmungsort gelieferte Ware zu verschaffen. Zusätzlich ist der Verkäufer verpflichtet, entweder einen Beförderungsvertrag abzuschließen oder einen solchen Vertrag zu verschaffen. Der Hinweis „zu verschaffen" bezieht sich hier auf mehrere hintereinander geschaltete Verkäufe in einer Verkaufskette („string sales"), die insbesondere im Rohstoffhandel vorkommen.

CIF kann ungeeignet sein, wenn die Ware dem Frachtführer übergeben wird, bevor sie sich auf dem Schiff befindet, z. B. bei containerisierter Ware, welche üblicherweise am Terminal geliefert wird. In derartigen Fällen sollte die CIP-Klausel verwendet werden.

CIF verpflichtet den Verkäufer, falls zutreffend, die Ware zur Ausfuhr freizumachen. Jedoch hat der Verkäufer keine Verpflichtung, die Ware zur Einfuhr freizumachen, Einfuhrzölle zu zahlen oder Einfuhrzollformalitäten zu erledigen.

A VERPFLICHTUNGEN DES VERKÄUFERS

A1 Allgemeine Verpflichtungen des Verkäufers

Der Verkäufer hat die Ware und die Handelsrechnung in Übereinstimmung mit dem Kaufvertrag bereitzustellen und jeden sonstigen vertraglich vereinbarten Konformitätsnachweis zu erbringen.

Jedes Dokument, auf das in **A1–A10** Bezug genommen wird, kann auch ein entsprechender elektronischer Beleg oder ein entsprechendes elektronisches Verfahren sein, wenn dies zwischen den Parteien vereinbart oder üblich ist.

A2 Lizenzen, Genehmigungen, Sicherheitsfreigaben und andere Formalitäten

Falls zutreffend, hat der Verkäufer auf eigene Gefahr und Kosten die Ausfuhrgenehmigung oder andere behördliche Genehmigungen zu beschaffen sowie alle Zollformalitäten zu erledigen, die für die Ausfuhr der Ware erforderlich sind.

A3 Beförderungs- und Versicherungsverträge

a. Beförderungsvertrag

Der Verkäufer muss einen Vertrag über die Beförderung der Ware von der gegebenenfalls vereinbarten Lieferstelle am Lieferort bis zum benannten Bestimmungshafen oder einer gegebenenfalls vereinbarten Stelle in diesem Hafen abschließen oder verschaffen. Der Beförderungsvertrag ist zu den üblichen Bedingungen auf Kosten des Verkäufers abzuschließen und hat die Beförderung auf der üblichen Route mit einem Schiff der Bauart zu gewährleisten, die normalerweise für den Transport der verkauften Warenart verwendet wird.

b. Versicherungsvertrag

Der Verkäufer hat auf eigene Kosten eine Transportversicherung abzuschließen, die zumindest der Mindestdeckung gemäß den Klauseln (C) der Institute Cargo Clauses (LMA/IUA) oder ähnlichen Klauseln entspricht. Die Versicherung ist bei Einzelversicherern oder Versicherungsgesellschaften mit einwandfreiem Leumund abzuschließen und muss den Käufer oder jede andere Person mit einem versicherbaren Interesse an der Ware berechtigen, Ansprüche direkt bei dem Versicherer geltend zu machen.

B VERPFLICHTUNGEN DES KÄUFERS

B1 Allgemeine Verpflichtungen des Käufers

Der Käufer hat den im Kaufvertrag genannten Preis der Ware zu zahlen.

Jedes Dokument, auf das in **B1–B10** Bezug genommen wird, kann auch ein entsprechender elektronischer Beleg oder ein entsprechendes elektronisches Verfahren sein, wenn dies zwischen den Parteien vereinbart oder üblich ist.

B2 Lizenzen, Genehmigungen, Sicherheitsfreigaben und andere Formalitäten

Falls zutreffend, obliegt es dem Käufer, auf eigene Gefahr und Kosten die Einfuhrgenehmigung oder andere behördliche Genehmigungen zu beschaffen sowie alle Zollformalitäten für die Einfuhr der Ware und für ihre Durchfuhr durch jedes Land zu erledigen.

B3 Beförderungs- und Versicherungsverträge

a. Beförderungsvertrag
Der Käufer hat gegenüber dem Verkäufer keine Verpflichtung, einen Beförderungsvertrag abzuschließen.

b. Versicherungsvertrag
Der Käufer hat gegenüber dem Verkäufer keine Verpflichtung, einen Versicherungsvertrag abzuschließen. Allerdings hat der Käufer dem Verkäufer auf dessen Verlangen alle für den Abschluss einer vom Käufer verlangten in **A3 b** vorgesehenen zusätzlichen Versicherung notwendigen Informationen zur Verfügung zu stellen.

Der Verkäufer muss auf Verlangen und Kosten des Käufers, vorbehaltlich der durch den Käufer zur Verfügung gestellten vom Verkäufer benötigten Informationen, zusätzliche Deckung, falls erhältlich, beschaffen, wie z.B. Deckung entsprechend den Klauseln (A) oder (B) der Institute Cargo Clauses (LMA/IUA) oder ähnlichen Klauseln und/oder der Institute War Clauses und/oder der Institute Strikes Clauses (LMA/IUA) oder ähnlichen Klauseln.

Die Versicherung muss zumindest den im Vertrag genannten Preis zuzüglich zehn Prozent (d.h. 110 %) decken und in der Währung des Vertrags ausgestellt sein.

Der Versicherungsschutz muss die Ware ab der Lieferstelle, wie in **A4** und **A5** festgelegt, bis mindestens zum benannten Bestimmungshafen decken.

Der Verkäufer hat dem Käufer die Versicherungspolice oder einen sonstigen Nachweis über den Versicherungsschutz zu übermitteln.

Ferner hat der Verkäufer dem Käufer auf dessen Verlangen, Gefahr und (gegebenenfalls entstehende) Kosten jene Informationen zur Verfügung zu stellen, die der Käufer für den Abschluss einer zusätzlichen Versicherung benötigt.

A4 Lieferung

Der Verkäufer hat die Ware zu liefern, entweder, indem er sie an Bord des Schiffs verbringt oder indem er die so gelieferte Ware verschafft. In beiden Fällen hat der Verkäufer die Ware zum vereinbarten Zeitpunkt oder innerhalb des vereinbarten Zeitraums und in der im Hafen üblichen Weise zu liefern.

A5 Gefahrenübergang

Der Verkäufer trägt bis zur Lieferung gemäß **A4** alle Gefahren des Verlustes oder der Beschädigung der Ware, mit Ausnahme von Verlust oder Beschädigung unter den in **B5** beschriebenen Umständen.

B4 Übernahme

Der Käufer muss die Ware übernehmen, wenn sie wie in **A4** vorgesehen geliefert worden ist, und sie von dem Frachtführer im benannten Bestimmungshafen entgegennehmen.

B5 Gefahrenübergang

Der Käufer trägt alle Gefahren des Verlustes oder der Beschädigung der Ware ab dem Zeitpunkt, an dem sie wie in **A4** vorgesehen geliefert worden ist.

Falls der Käufer es unterlässt, gemäß **B7** zu benachrichtigen, trägt er alle Gefahren des Verlustes oder der Beschädigung der Ware ab dem für die Verschiffung vereinbarten Zeitpunkt oder ab Ablauf der hierfür vereinbarten Frist, vorausgesetzt, die Ware ist eindeutig als die vertragliche Ware kenntlich gemacht worden.

A6 Kostenverteilung

Der Verkäufer hat zu tragen

a. alle die Ware betreffenden Kosten bis diese gemäß **A4** geliefert worden ist, ausgenommen solcher Kosten, die wie in **B6** vorgesehen vom Käufer zu tragen sind;

b. die Fracht und alle anderen aus **A3 a** entstehenden Kosten einschließlich der Kosten für die Verladung der Ware an Bord und alle Entladekosten im vereinbarten Entladehafen, die nach dem Beförderungsvertrag vom Verkäufer zu tragen sind;

c. die aus **A3 b** resultierenden Kosten für die Versicherung; und

d. falls zutreffend, die Kosten der für die Ausfuhr notwendigen Zollformalitäten sowie alle Zölle, Steuern und andere Abgaben, die bei der Ausfuhr fällig werden, und die Kosten für die Durchfuhr der Ware durch jedes Land, soweit diese nach dem Beförderungsvertrag vom Verkäufer zu tragen sind.

B6 Kostenverteilung

Der Käufer hat, vorbehaltlich der Bestimmungen in **A3 a**, zu tragen

a. alle die Ware betreffenden Kosten ab dem Zeitpunkt, an dem sie wie in **A4** vorgesehen geliefert worden ist, ausgenommen, falls zutreffend, die Kosten der für die Ausfuhr notwendigen Zollformalitäten sowie alle Zölle, Steuern und andere in **A6 d** genannte Abgaben, die bei der Ausfuhr fällig werden;

b. alle die Ware betreffenden Kosten und Abgaben während des Transports bis zu ihrer Ankunft im Bestimmungshafen, es sei denn, solche Kosten und Abgaben gehen gemäß dem Beförderungsvertrag zu Lasten des Verkäufers;

c. die Entladekosten, einschließlich Kosten für Leichterung und Kaigebühren, es sei denn, diese Kosten und Abgaben sind nach dem Beförderungsvertrag vom Verkäufer zu tragen;

d. alle zusätzlichen Kosten, sollte er die Benachrichtigung gemäß **B7** unterlassen, ab dem für die Verschiffung vereinbarten Zeitpunkt oder ab Ablauf der hierfür vereinbarten Frist, vorausgesetzt, die Ware ist eindeutig als die vertragliche Ware kenntlich gemacht worden;

e. falls zutreffend, alle Zölle, Steuern und andere Abgaben sowie die Kosten der Zollformalitäten, die bei der Einfuhr der Ware und, soweit nicht im Beförderungsvertrag enthalten, bei ihrer Durchfuhr durch jedes Land anfallen; und

f. die Kosten für jede zusätzlich auf Verlangen des Käufers gemäß **A3 b** und **B3 b** abgeschlossene Versicherung.

A7 Benachrichtigungen an den Käufer

Der Verkäufer hat den Käufer über alles Nötige zu benachrichtigen, damit dieser die üblicherweise notwendigen Maßnahmen zur Übernahme der Ware treffen kann.

A8 Transportdokument

Der Verkäufer hat auf eigene Kosten dem Käufer unverzüglich das übliche Transportdokument für den vereinbarten Bestimmungshafen zur Verfügung zu stellen.

Dieses Transportdokument muss über die vertragliche Ware lauten, ein innerhalb der für die Verschiffung vereinbarten Frist liegendes Datum tragen, den Käufer berechtigen, die Herausgabe der Ware im Bestimmungshafen von dem Frachtführer zu verlangen und, sofern nichts anderes vereinbart wurde, es dem Käufer ermöglichen, die Ware während des Transports an einen nachfolgenden Käufer durch Übertragung des Dokuments oder durch Mitteilung an den Frachtführer zu verkaufen.

Wird ein solches Transportdokument als begebbares Dokument und in mehreren Originalen ausgestellt, muss ein vollständiger Satz von Originalen dem Käufer übergeben werden.

A9 Prüfung – Verpackung – Kennzeichnung

Der Verkäufer hat die Kosten jener Prüfvorgänge (wie Qualitätsprüfung, Messen, Wiegen und Zählen), die notwendig sind, um die Ware gemäß **A4** zu liefern, sowie die Kosten für alle von den Behörden des Ausfuhrlandes angeordneten Warenkontrollen vor der Verladung (pre-shipment inspection) zu tragen.

Der Verkäufer hat auf eigene Kosten die Ware zu verpacken, es sei denn, es ist handelsüblich, die jeweilige Art der verkauften Ware unverpackt zu transportieren. Der Verkäufer kann die Ware in der für ihren Transport geeigneten Weise verpacken, es sei denn, der Käufer hat den Verkäufer vor Vertragsschluss über spezifische Verpackungsanforderungen in Kenntnis gesetzt. Die Verpackung ist in geeigneter Weise zu kennzeichnen.

B7 Benachrichtigungen an den Verkäufer

Wann immer der Käufer berechtigt ist, den Zeitpunkt für die Verschiffung der Ware und/oder die Stelle für die Entgegennahme der Ware innerhalb des benannten Bestimmungshafens zu bestimmen, hat er den Verkäufer in angemessener Weise darüber zu benachrichtigen.

B8 Liefernachweis

Der Käufer hat das wie in **A8** vorgesehen zur Verfügung gestellte Transportdokument anzunehmen, wenn dieses mit dem Vertrag übereinstimmt.

B9 Prüfung der Ware

Der Käufer hat die Kosten für jede vor der Verladung zwingend erforderliche Warenkontrolle (pre-shipment inspection) zu tragen, mit Ausnahme behördlich angeordneter Kontrollen des Ausfuhrlandes.

A10 Unterstützung bei Informationen und damit verbundene Kosten

Der Verkäufer hat, falls zutreffend, dem Käufer auf dessen Verlangen, Gefahr und Kosten rechtzeitig alle Dokumente und Informationen, einschließlich sicherheitsrelevanter Informationen, die der Käufer für die Einfuhr der Ware und/oder für ihren Transport bis zum endgültigen Bestimmungsort benötigt, zur Verfügung zu stellen oder ihn bei deren Beschaffung zu unterstützen.

Der Verkäufer hat dem Käufer alle Kosten und Abgaben zu erstatten, die dem Käufer durch das Zurverfügungstellen oder die Unterstützung bei der Beschaffung der in **B10** vorgesehenen Dokumente und Informationen entstanden sind.

B10 Unterstützung bei Informationen und damit verbundene Kosten

Der Käufer hat dem Verkäufer rechtzeitig alle sicherheitsrelevanten Informationsanforderungen mitzuteilen, so dass der Verkäufer die Verpflichtungen entsprechend **A10** erfüllen kann.

Der Käufer hat dem Verkäufer alle Kosten und Abgaben zu erstatten, die dem Verkäufer durch das Zurverfügungstellen oder die Unterstützung bei der Beschaffung der Dokumente und Informationen wie in **A10** vorgesehen entstanden sind.

Der Käufer hat, falls zutreffend, dem Verkäufer rechtzeitig auf dessen Verlangen, Gefahr und Kosten alle Dokumente und Informationen, einschließlich sicherheitsrelevanter Informationen, die der Verkäufer für den Transport und die Ausfuhr der Ware sowie für ihre Durchfuhr durch jedes Land benötigt, zur Verfügung zu stellen oder ihn bei deren Beschaffung zu unterstützen.

ANHANG

DIE ICC AUF EINEN BLICK

Die private Wirtschaft benötigt eine starke Stimme, um ihre Ansichten global gegenüber zwischenstaatlichen Organisationen erfolgreich vertreten zu können. Die Internationale Handelskammer (International Chamber of Commerce, ICC), mit Hauptsitz in Paris, ist die branchenübergreifende Vertretung der Weltwirtschaft und Dialogpartner gegenüber internationalen Institutionen und nationalen Regierungen.

Vorrangige Ziele der 1919 gegründeten ICC sind die Förderung eines freien, fairen und grenzüberschreitenden Handels sowie die Unterstützung von Unternehmen bei der Bewältigung der Globalisierung.

Dienstleister für die Wirtschaft
Die ICC ermöglicht durch von ihr entwickelte Vertragsregeln und Richtlinien sowie über ihren Internationalen Schiedsgerichtshof eine effiziente Abwicklung internationaler Geschäfte.

Internationale Interessensvertretung der Wirtschaft
Die ICC vertritt als Stimme der Weltwirtschaft deren Interessen gegenüber internationalen Organisationen wie beispielsweise den Vereinten Nationen (UN) und der Welthandelsorganisation (WTO). Auch bei bedeutenden informellen Zusammenschlüssen wie G20 und G8 verschafft sie sich Gehör.

Vordenker für die Wirtschaft
Freier und fairer Welthandel ist eine wichtige Grundlage für Frieden, Sicherheit und Wohlstand. Doch gilt es auch, sich mit den Begleiterscheinungen der Globalisierung auseinanderzusetzen. Diese Rolle nimmt die ICC seit jeher wahr.

Der Einfluss der ICC rund um den Globus beruht auf dem weltweiten Netzwerk ihrer Nationalkomitees, die in mehr als 90 Ländern zu finden sind. Darüber hinaus hat die ICC Direktmitglieder in weiteren 34 Ländern. Die Aufgabe der Nationalkomitees ist es, sich bei den nationalen Regierungen für die Interessen der Wirtschaft einzusetzen sowie Beiträge für die strategische Arbeit der ICC zu liefern.

Die deutsche Vertretung der ICC

Das deutsche Nationalkomitee der Internationalen Handelskammer ist die ICC Deutschland. Sie ist zum einen Bindeglied zwischen den deutschen Mitgliedern – Unternehmen, Verbänden, Industrie- und Handelskammern – und der ICC-Zentrale in Paris und setzt sich dort für deren Belange ein. Zum anderen kommuniziert sie die Positionen der ICC gegenüber den Ansprechpartnern der deutschen Bundesregierung, die ihrerseits auf Entscheidungen internationaler Institutionen wie beispielsweise UN oder WTO Einfluss nehmen.

In ihrer Struktur ist die ICC Deutschland gegliedert in Präsidium, Hauptausschuss sowie Geschäftsführung, die ihren Sitz in Berlin hat.

Weitere Informationen finden Sie unter **www.icc-deutschland.de**.

ICC-STREITBEILEGUNG

Die Einbeziehung einer oder mehrerer Incoterms® Klauseln führt nicht zu einer automatischen Anwendbarkeit der ICC-Streitbeilegungsverfahren. Die Vertragsparteien, die im Streitfall die ICC-Streitbeilegungsregeln nutzen möchten, sollten deswegen eine eindeutige und klare diesbezügliche Vereinbarung treffen. Zu diesem Zweck bietet die ICC vorformulierte Standardklauseln an, welche die Parteien in ihre Verträge aufnehmen können. Sollte der Vertrag eine solche Klausel nicht enthalten, können die Parteien sich auch nachträglich auf die Anwendung der ICC-Streitbeilegungsregeln einigen.

Die ICC bietet eine große Anzahl von Streitbeilegungsverfahren an, um Parteien bei der effektiven Beilegung ihrer Streitigkeiten zu helfen. Die ICC-Streitbeilegungsverfahren gehen auf unterschiedlichste Anforderungen und Bedürfnisse ein. Jedem Streitbeilegungsverfahren liegt ein eigenes Regelwerk zugrunde. Kulturelle, sprachliche und rechtliche Besonderheiten sowie branchenübliche Usancen werden berücksichtigt.

Schiedsgerichtsbarkeit: Sie führt zu einem bindenden Schiedsspruch, der von einem aus einem oder drei Schiedsrichtern bestehendem Schiedsgericht erlassen wird. Der Internationale Schiedsgerichtshof der ICC verwaltet dieses Verfahren. Der Schiedsspruch ist in einer großen Anzahl von Ländern vollstreckbar, da die ICC-Schiedsgerichtsbarkeit rechtliche Anerkennung in den meisten Handelsnationen der Welt findet.

Einvernehmliche Streitbeilegung in einem **Amicable Dispute Resolution Verfahren (ADR),** insbesondere **Mediation:** Unter den ADR-Regeln können die Parteien zwischen verschiedenen Streitbeilegungstechniken wählen, um zu einer einvernehmlichen Beilegung ihres Konflikts zu gelangen. Die Parteien haben die Möglichkeit, diejenige Regelungstechnik zu wählen, die ihrer Ansicht nach am besten zu einer Einigung führen wird, zum Beispiel *Mediation, Neutral Evaluation, Mini-Trial* oder eine Kombination verschiedener Techniken.

ICC Dispute Boards: Sie werden bereits ab Beginn für die gesamte vereinbarte Vertragslaufzeit gebildet, um zwischen den Vertragsparteien Streitigkeiten frühzeitig beilegen zu können. Es werden verschiedene Arten von ICC Dispute Boards angeboten, je nachdem, welche Kompetenzen die Parteien den Mitgliedern des Boards einräumen möchten.

ICC-Sachverständigenverfahren: In diesem Verfahren wünschen die Parteien, dass ein neutraler Sachverständiger ein Gutachten über die streitige Frage verfasst. Zu diesem Zweck kann die ICC einen Sachverständigen aus dem entsprechenden Bereich vorschlagen oder benennen. Die zu beurteilenden Sachfragen können aus sämtlichen Bereichen stammen, z. B. Technik, Finanzen oder Recht. Die angebotenen Dienste decken die Suche nach einem geeigneten Sachverständigen bis hin zur vollständigen Betreuung eines Sachverständigenverfahrens ab.

DOCDEX: Dieses Verfahren wird zur schnellen und kostengünstigen Beilegung von Streitigkeiten im Zusammenhang mit Dokumenten-Akkreditiven, Rembours zwischen Banken, Inkassi und Bankgarantien angeboten.

Für weitere Informationen, einschließlich aller einschlägigen Regeln und Klauseln, besuchen Sie bitte die Internetseite von ICC Dispute Resolution Services: **www.iccadr.org**.

IMPRESSUM

veröffentlicht im September 2010 durch

ICC Deutschland e. V.
Wilhelmstr. 43 G
10117 Berlin

ICC-Publikation 715 ED
ISBN 978-3-929621-71-6

ICC Deutschland
Internationale Handelskammer
The world business organization

www.icc-deutschland.de
Tel. +49 (0) 30 200 73 63 00

Diese Publikation ist auch zu beziehen über

ICC Austria
Internationale Handelskammer
The world business organisation

www.icc-austria.org
Tel. +43 (0) 1 50105 3716

ICC Switzerland
International Chamber of Commerce
The world business organization

www.icc-switzerland.ch
Tel. +41 (0) 44 421 34 50